William Shakespeare

Merchant of Venice

Edited by

Randall Martin

Commentary by

Peter Lichtenfels

The Applause Shakespeare Library
Merchant of Venice

Edited by Randall Martin
Commentary by Peter Lichtenfels
General Series Editor: John Russell Brown

Library of Congress Cataloging-in-Publication Data

Library of Congress Card Number: 00-111097

British Library Cataloging-in-Publication Data
A catalog record for this book is available from the British Library.

ISBN: 1-55783-388-5

APPLAUSE THEATRE BOOKS
151 W46th Street, 8th Floor
New York, NY 10036
Phone: (212) 575-9265
FAX: (646) 562-5852
email: info@applausepub.com

COMBINED BOOK SERVICES LTD.
Units I/K, Paddock Wood Distribution Centre
Paddock Wood, Tonbridge, Kent TN 12 6UU
Phone: (44) 01892 837171
Fax: (44) 01892 837272

SALES & DISTRIBUTION, HAL LEONARD CORP.
7777 West Bluemound Road, P.O. Box 13819
Milwaukee, WI 53213
Phone: (414) 774-3630
Fax: (414) 774-3259
email: halinfo@halleonard.com
internet: www.halleonard.com

Table of Contents

Other Titles in the Applause Shakespeare Library:

King Lear
Macbeth
A Midsummer Night's Dream
The Tempest
Twelfth Night
Othello
Romeo and Juliet
Antony and Cleopatra
Measure for Measure

General Preface to the Applause Shakespeare Library

This edition is designed to help readers see and hear the plays in action. It gives an impression of how actors can bring life to the text and shows how certain speeches, movements, or silences take on huge importance once the words have left the page and become part of a performance. It is a theatrical edition, like no other available at this time.

Everyone knows that Shakespeare wrote for performance and not for solitary readers or students in classrooms. Yet the great problem of how to publish the plays so that readers can understand their theatrical life is only beginning to be tackled. Various solutions have been tried. The easiest—and it is an uneasy compromise—is to commission some director or leading actor to write a preface about the play in performance and print that at the beginning of the volume, followed by a critical and historical introduction, the text and notes about verbal difficulties, a textual introduction, and a collation of variant reading as in any other edition. Another easy answer is to supply extensive stage directions to sort out how characters enter or exit and describe any gestures or actions that the text explicitly requires. Both methods give the reader little or no help in realizing the play in performance, moment by moment, as the text is read.

A more thorough-going method is to include some notes about staging and acting among the annotations of meaning, topical references, classical allusions, textual problems, and so forth. The snag here is that the theatrical details make no consecutive sense and cannot deal with the larger issues of the build-up of conflict or atmosphere, the developing impression of character, or the effect of group and individual movement on stage. Such notes offer, at best, intermittent assistance.

In the more expensive one-volume editions, with larger-than-usual formats, yet another method is used to include a stage history of the play showing how other ages have staged the play and describing a few recent productions that have been more than usually successful with the critics. The snag here is that unavailable historical knowledge is required to interpret records of earlier performances. Moreover, the journalistic accounts of productions which are quoted in these histories are liable to emphasize what is unusual in a production rather than the opportunities offered to actors in any production of the play, the text's enduring theatrical vitality. In any case, all this material is kept separate from the rest of the book and not easily consulted during a reading of the text.

The Applause Shakespeare goes further than any of these. It does the usual tasks expected of a responsible, modern edition, but adds a very special feature: a continuous commentary on the text by a professional director or a leading actor that considers the stage life of the play as its action unfolds. It shows what is demanded from the actors—line by line where necessary—and points out what decisions about interpretation have to be made and the consequences of one choice over another. It indicates where emotional climaxes are placed—and where conflicting thoughts in the character's mind create subtextual pressures beneath the words. Visual statements are noted: the effect of groups of figures on stages, of an isolated figure, or of a pair of linked figures in a changing relationship; the effect of delayed or unexpected entries, sudden departures, slow or processional exuents, or a momentarily empty stage. Everything that happens on stage comes within the notice of this commentary. A reader can "feel" what the play would be like in action.

What the commentary does not do is equally important from the reader's point of view. It does not try to provide a single theatrical reading of the text. Rather if offers a range of possibilities, a number of suggestions as to what an actor might do. Performances cannot be confined to a single, unalterable realization: rather, each production is continually discovering new potential in a text, and it is this power of revelation and revaluation that the commentary of the Applause Shakespeare seeks to open up to individual readers. With this text in hand, the play can be produced in the theatre of the mind, creating a performance suitable to the moment and responsive to individual imaginations. As stimulus for such recreations, the commentary sometimes describes the choices that particular actors or directors made in famous productions, showing what effect words or physical performances have achieved. The purpose here is to supplement what a reader might supply from his or her own experience and imagination, and also to suggest ways in which further research might discover more about the text's theatrical life.

The commentary is printed in a wide column on the page facing the text itself, so that reference can be quickly made at any particular point or, alternatively, so that the commentary can be read as its own narrative of the pay in action. Also, to the right of the text are explanations of difficult words, puns, multiple meanings, topical allusions, references to other texts, etc. All of these things will be found in other editions, but here it is readily accessible without the eye having to seek out the foot of the page or notes bunched together at the rear of the volume. The text is modernized in spelling. Both stage directions and punctuation are kept to a minimum—enough to make reading easy, but not so elaborate that readers are prevented from giving life to the text in whatever way they choose. As an aid to reading aloud, speech-prefixes are printed in full and extra space used to set speeches apart from each other; when the text is read silently, each new voice can register clearly. At the rear of the book, an extended note explains the authority for the text and a collation gives details of variant readings and emendations.

In many ways the Applause Shakespeare is a pioneering edition, responding to an old challenge in a new way and trying to break down barriers to understanding that have proved very obstinate for a long time. Further volumes are in preparation and editorial procedures are being kept under review. Reports on the usefulness of the edition, and especially of its theatrical commentary, would be most welcome. Please write to John Russell Brown, c/o Applause Books, 151 West 46th Street, 8th Floor, New York, NY 10036.

Acknowledgements

Though nearly ten years have passed between the time of finishing this edition and writing these acknowledgements to accompany its publication, the memory of those who generously provided me with information and assistance remains fresh. Anybody who researches *The Merchant's* stage life quickly becomes aware of the critical imbalance that exists between discussions of its two leading characters. While Shylock is conventionally regarded as the play's main concern, he actually has less than half the number of lines of Portia; and whereas studies of his role are many and searching, those for Portia have been relatively few. When preparing this edition I therefore decided to give her part more attention than usual in my introduction. Further, I discussed playing Portia with several actresses to find out how they felt about taking up the role today. It became apparent that they approach her part with considerable ambivalence, owing to Portia's complicity in destroying Shylock and her difficulty in establishing a position outside the play's morally compromised discourses of race and gender. Accordingly, many actresses no longer view Portia as a plum role, as previous generations of performers generally did, nor do they generally share the views of literary critics of the 1970s and 80s, who assess her actions more positively as self-affirming responses to patriarchal repression. My first thanks are therefore due to Dame Judi Dench, Deborah Findley, Lisa Harrow, and Seanna McKenna, who kindly answered my enquiries and made themselves available to discuss their performances. Their responses provided me with a range of contemporary reactions to Portia, from outright aversion to grudging admiration, and deepened my own understanding and presentation of the play.

During the course of my research, the staff of many libraries have been unfailingly helpful in answering my enquires and placing original performance documents at my disposal. I am particularly indebted to: Mrs W.A. Weare of The Ellen Terry Memorial Museum, Smallhythe, Kent; Marian Pringle and Sylvia Morris of the Shakespeare Centre Library, Stratford-upon-Avon; and Andrew Kirk of the Theatre Museum Library, London. The following institutions graciously allowed me to consult and quote from their material: The Edwin Booth Collection, New York; the Library of The Garrick Club, London; the Theatre Collection of the New York Public Library; the Theatre Museum Library, London; The Shakespeare Centre, Stratford-upon-Avon; and the Bodleian Library.

Finally, I am very grateful to the series editor, John Russell Brown, for providing me with generous criticism, encouraging advice, and illuminating recollections of many of the productions described in the following pages.

Randall Martin
Fredericton, New Brunswick

INTRODUCTION

Performances of *The Merchant of Venice* take place nowadays in a peculiar atmosphere of popular appeal and critical disrepute. Audiences are attracted to the many productions staged every year by the enduring power of the play's central conflict, which invites them to enter into imaginative alliance with the characters of Venice and Belmont as they confront Shylock's malicious threats. They likewise come for the exoticism and spectacle which has made Venice legendary, that mingling of "Oriental" and European cultures evocative of luminous art, colorful masquerades, and magnificent architecture, all once sustained by lucrative trade in silks and spices. Even today when financial restraint holds sway in most public theatres, productions can rarely resist conjuring up some of this visual splendor through the use of grand sets and gorgeous costumes.

But because *The Merchant of Venice* contains objectionable social attitudes, it is also deeply controversial. The play's realistic portrayal of Shylock's essential humanity and his ordeal as a Jew living in a Christian society demonstrates that Shakespeare was able to see beyond racial stereotypes. But distaste for the story's antisemitic assumptions, now inevitably associated with attitudes that culminated in the Holocaust, threatens both its stage-worthiness and Shakespeare's fame as a dramatic genius. And since in the end Shylock is not only defeated but also (unlike his source-story) degraded as an alien, Shakespeare seems to leave himself open to charges of intellectual dishonesty, or at the least of a regrettable lapse in imaginative sympathy.

Yet overall the play's critical reputation has been shaped by stage performance as well as literary assessment, by which directors and actors are continually reinterpreting its notorious conflicts—reinterpretations inherently more successful in overturning settled notions of what the play is about. Since the eighteenth century actors have approached it in many different ways, with performances of Shylock determining the tone and thematic approach of most productions. Although he appears in only five scenes, Shylock habitually dominates the play. His role's expressive possibilities anticipate those of Shakespeare's great tragic heros, and have served to establish the reputations of many renowned actors, few of whom have been content to play him as a minor, one-dimensional villain. Instead they focus on the anguish Shylock experiences, finding in his "sufferance" as a Jew among Christians a profound capacity to generate audience sympathy. When presented this way Shylock becomes a victim and, in certain productions, a universal symbol of racial persecution and social ostracism. Theatrical performance has therefore decisively influenced the play's critical reception by turning its potentially offensive treatment of Shylock into an arraignment of the Christians' intolerance and brutality. Moreover, uncovering compassion for Shylock suggests that Shakespeare did manage successfully to transcend his own age's prejudices in writing a far-sighted plea for tolerance. The casualty of this revisionism, however, is the play's intended comedy, in terms of both humour and its happy ending. Centering attention on Shylock's struggle with the Venetians often entails cutting or debasing the romance episodes in which Bassanio successfully woos Portia. Indeed nineteenth-century productions made it customary to cut all of Act V—the lovers' celebratory return to Belmont and the restoration of Antonio's wealth—in order to concentrate emotional responses exclusively on Shylock.

Since *The Merchant's* cultural significance has been particularly affected by its life in the theatre, taking account of important performances is a useful way to begin thinking about the play. Broadly speaking, they tend to treat it in one of two ways, each corresponding to a different dramatic genre: either as romantic comedy, where Portia and ideals associated with Belmont redeem Venice, and where securing the lovers' happiness demands the defeat of Shylock, or as ironic comedy, often aspiring to tragedy, where responses are concentrated on his abuse by the Venetians. Neither of these categories is of course rigid or absolute, and within each there are considerable degrees of variation. But starting a discussion in terms of either dominantly comic or tragic action will bring the play's major themes and conflicts into sharp focus, and also isolate those key interpretative decisions actors must make in performance.

Comedy

The Merchant of Venice belongs to a group of comedies Shakespeare wrote in the 1590s which are customarily described as romantic or festive. They celebrate courtship in stories about young lovers who have to overcome particular social and parental objections to obtain marriage partners of their choice. In *The Merchant* such obstacles are raised by Shylock, a Jewish moneylender and father of one of the lovers, and by the end of the play three couples join together in triumph over him. In a symbolic way comic productions also suggest that positive social values represented by the "good" characters are opposed to a range of antisocial ones personified by Shylock: Antonio's generosity to Shylock's "thrift," Bassanio's love to Shylock's hatred, Jessica's willing assimilation to his defiant apartness, Portia's creative insight to his self-destructive literalism. Attitudes on each side of this divide are associated with two corresponding locales: Venice is a rich society filled with fierce commercial rivalry and emotional anxiety: Belmont is also rich but idealized as a haven of munificence and repose. Such a pattern of oppositions is reassuringly familiar to most audiences, though this does not imply it is naïve, or that comic productions are not obliged to make textual changes to keep it clear-cut.

Shakespeare's narrative combines two ancient folktales within this moral framework. In one an evil moneylender threatens to cut a pound of flesh as forfeit from a borrower who defaults in repaying a loan. At the last moment, however, a woman disguised as a lawyer finds that the contract makes no provision for shedding blood and so defeats the moneylender. Among the several versions of this story available to Shakespeare, he most likely consulted *Il Pecorone* ("The Big Sheep" or "Fool"), a collection of stories written in Italian by Ser Giovanni Fiorentino and published in Milan in 1558 (Shakespeare presumably read them in the original). The second folktale appeared in the *Gesta Romanorum*, printed in English in 1577 and again in 1595, and takes the form of a moral test: a lover must confront three chests of gold, silver and lead, and choose the one which best represents his lady to win her. In Shakespeare's play the lady is Portia and the riddle part of her dead father's will, imposed upon prospective suitors to protect her and her inherited wealth from mere fortune-hunters.

Bassanio is the third of the play's suitors who "ventures" the casket-riddle, and risks the penalty of perpetual celibacy if he chooses wrongly. He does so not only for typically romantic reasons—because Portia is beautiful and virtuous—but also because she represents a means of repaying the debts he has run up by living extravagantly. In this respect Bassanio takes on associations with the Prodigal Son (Luke 15) shared by his counterpart Giannetto in *Il Pecorone*. In the biblical account the Prodigal Son is eventually forgiven and prospers in spite of his wasteful career. Bassanio's relation to the story suggests that although we should not be uncritical of his mixed motives, we are ultimately meant to side with the "hedonism of spending" represented by him and his friends against Shylock's "asceticism of hoarding" (Levin, 15).

To reach Belmont and woo Portia in proper style, Bassanio must approach his close friend Antonio, the merchant of the play's title, about obtaining a loan on his behalf. As the play opens Antonio is suffering from a mysterious depression which may be related to Bassanio's hints that he intends to seek a wife. To indicate the depth of his friendship Antonio risks entering into an apparently jesting ("merry") bond with his enemy Shylock; this entitles Shylock to claim a pound of Antonio's flesh if the loan is not repaid on time. Thus when Bassanio arrives in Belmont to "hazard" the caskets, the occasion signifies Antonio's opportunity to show his unqualified devotion towards Bassanio, as well as Bassanio's personal gamble to win Portia. Solving the riddle accordingly places Bassanio in a situation of conflicting loyalties, which Portia must correct through the ring-test in act five by establishing the priority of her claims as a wife over Antonio's as a friend.

At the heart of the casket-choice is a paradox: to win the "richly left" Portia, Bassanio must recognize the spiritual emptiness of the gold that gets him to Belmont and which he will share as her husband, and in turn acknowledge that only Portia's love has real value. Her father's will thus tests suitors according to the Christian precept of subordinating worldly wealth to spiritual enrichment. Whereas the first two suitors Morocco and Aragon choose by "fleshly" standards—material and social status—Bassanio realizes that choosing according to Portia's inner worth must entail risking the loss of all he owns. When Antonio's ships later fail to return and he is endangered by Shylock's bond, Portia uses the same anti-material reasoning to save Antonio: by outwitting Shylock she demonstrates the value of living according to humane principles of mercy and charity over strict adherence to legal rules.

Traditional comic productions of *The Merchant* either implicitly or explicitly endorse these ideals by stressing the serious purpose behind the casket-choice, and by giving the trial in IV.i. overtones of a philosophical debate, with Portia representing compassion and generosity against Shylock's implacable eye-for-an-eye reciprocity. An actress's tone will convey approval in Portia's vow, "If I live to be as old as Sibylla, I will die as chaste as Diana, unless I be obtained by the manner of my father's will" (I.ii.105-7), rather than suggesting the whole business is a nuisance. And while Morocco and Aragon can safely be played as comically absurd, Bassanio's choice in III.ii. is usually staged as a solemn moment, sometimes conveying a religious atmosphere. In William Poel's 1898 production, to take an extreme example, the three caskets were set upon an altar accompanied by a priest, candle-bearing acolytes, and organ music. Actresses will also make Portia's famous plea for mercy (IV.i.180-201) appear to be the focus of the Christians' whole value-system.

This does not go unquestioned, however, since Shylock's antipathy towards Antonio and the other Venetians is given tremendous dramatic urgency because he is a wronged Jew. Here Shakespeare's portrayal was influenced by Christopher Marlowe's *The Jew of Malta* (1589) and its villain-hero Barabbas. Barabbas actually bears little resemblance to Shylock or any real Jew, being instead a fantastic creation whose spectacular crimes against Christians even more corrupt than himself represents a typically Marlovian fling at conventional morality. But he gives us an idea of the kind of distorted image Shakespeare was responding to in his more complex portrait of Shylock. Furthermore Marlowe's play was revived in 1594 a few years before Shakespeare wrote *The Merchant* (1596-8) to capitalize on anti-Jewish feelings aroused by the trial and execution of Dr Roderigo Lopez. Except for a tiny London community living as outwardly conforming Christians, Jews were virtually unknown in England, though in the popular European imagination they were accused of anti-Christian atrocities. Dr Lopez, who was a Portuguese Jew, probably fell victim to these fantasies when he was found guilty on trumped-up charges of attempting to poison Queen Elizabeth and hanged before cheering crowds. The affair stimulated topical interest in a revival of *The Jew of Malta* and enflamed popular anti-semitism, which presumably lingered to greet Shylock several years later.

Unfortunately we have only the slimmest early evidence of performance. The original edition's title page, printed in 1600, claims it was acted several times by Shakespeare's company, the Lord Chamberlain's Men, and we know it was performed twice at court before James I in 1605. No other reliable record exists until 1701, when George Granville adapted Shakespeare's play, partly to make Shylock more comic. He was played by the popular "low" comedian Thomas Doggett, who probably mimicked the personal habits of certain notorious London moneylenders. Shylock's role was not taken seriously after this until 1741 when Charles Macklin restored Shakespeare's text in a production which held the stage for nearly 50 years. Macklin made Shylock the embodiment of malignant revenge:

> Upon the entrance of Anthonio, the Jew makes the audience acquainted with his motives of antipathy against the Merchant [I.iii.34ff]. Mr. Macklin had no sooner delivered this speech, than the audience suddenly burst out into a thunder of applause, and in proportion as he afterwards proceeded to exhibit and mark the malevolence, the villainy, and the diabolical atrocity of the character, so in proportion did the admiring and delighted audience testify their approbation...(Kirkman, i, 258-9)

Shylock was ferocious during the street scenes (III.i. and iii.) and grimly sinister in the courtroom (IV.i.). Audiences responded approvingly to his portrayal of a hateful monster who confirmed their deep-rooted distrust: "the sight of this Jew suffices to awaken at once, in the best-regulated mind, all the prejudices of childhood against this people" (Furness, 374). Macklin's savagery also strengthened audience identification with the victorious Christians after Shylock's downfall, thus throwing the play's final comic phase into high relief.

Like Macklin the nineteenth-century American actor Edwin Booth presented Shylock as a deadly menace, though he yielded to the fashion of contemporary tragic productions by playing Shylock for pathos when he finally left the courtroom. Booth believed Shylock's evil was motivated chiefly by avarice rather than racial hatred (Lelyveld, 68); thus even when learning about Jessica's sale of Leah's turquoise for a monkey—a moment which usually never fails to humanize Shylock in the theatre—Booth's Shylock seemed concerned only about the financial loss. From his entrance in I.iii. his fingers kept "ever moving as if from the constant habit of caressing and feeling the ducats that are passing through them," while during the aside revealing his "ancient grudge" against Antonio he trembled with hatred. Like all actors performing Shylock, Booth's suggestion of the exact moment when Shylock decides in earnest to use the "merry bond" to kill Antonio was crucial. As in many comic productions it came early in I.iii, when "by expression and gesture he denote[d] the coming of the idea and a sudden resolve," but immediately covered up with "a fawning, half-jocular tone."[1] Indicating Shylock's deadly seriousness from the very beginning also usually leads actors to make him psychologically consistent in the scenes which follow, even though Shakespeare's text (for instance at II.v. when Shylock leaves his home in Jessica's care) can add conflicting aspects to his personality. Except for passionate outrage in III.i, Booth's brooding Shylock waited with the

> awful composure of inherent evil which may be noted in the observant stillness of a deadly reptile, aware of its potency and in no haste, although unalterably determined, to make use of it. (Winter, Booth, 384)

Booth's was typical of many lesser nineteenth-century productions in that his extensive textual editing made the play a comedy only in terms of the trial's outcome, not its overall effect. Morocco and Aragon disappeared from the Belmont scenes, while the final curtain came down as Gratiano hissed Shylock from the court. The romance quality of Bassanio and Portia's courtship suffered from cuts to metaphorical passages depicting him as a "Jason" and "Hercules," and her as a legendary prize ("Golden Fleece") and endangered sacrifice (Hesione). Indeed the shrinking of Portia's role rendered her nearly as mute as the pictorial scenery around her, so that not even accomplished actresses playing opposite Booth such as Charlotte Cushman and Anna Modjeska achieved much success with the part.

Although similar treatments of the play continued in American and English productions well into this century, other directors sought ways of reviving what they thought to be the real comic spirit of Shakespeare's original. In 1898 William Poel's Elizabethan Stage Society tried an academic approach, producing the play under "authentic" seventeenth-century stage conditions: a bare stage except for essential hand props, more natural delivery of lines, non-illusionist acting, and an uninterrupted flow of action between scenes. Though many of Poel's innovations were timely corrections of Victorian extravagance, he also assumed Shakespeare's Shylock was kin to that which seventeenth-century reports ascribe to Richard Burbage: a red-wigged buffoon playing the role for slapstick. Poel also tried to reverse the tradition of making Shylock tragic by staging the action so as to coerce audiences into siding with the Christians; for example he underplayed Shylock's "I pray you give me leave to go from hence,/I am not well" (IV.i.391-2) and had him rush from the court in a ludicrous rage to prevent any last-minute feeling of pity.

Successfully reclaiming the play's comedy had to wait for Theodore Komisarjevsky's startling production of July 1929. Like Poel he too went back historically but this time in a "fantasticated" way to the festive spirit of Venetian Carnival. His approach grew out of those episodes concerning the Gobbos and the elopement of Jessica and Lorenzo inspired by Italian intrigue comedy which Shakespeare had experimented with earlier in *The Comedy of Errors* and *The Taming of the Shrew*. For *The Merchant,* Shakespeare may have also consulted Anthony Munday's *Zelauto or The Fountain of Fame* (1580), a romance which builds upon the flesh-bond folktale by having several lovers use trickery and disguise to outwit a miserly father and a menacing usurer. Through certain characters' costumes and gestures Komisarjevsky also brought out the play's associations with Italian *Commedia dell'Arte*, Launcelot Gobbo recalling the Zany, Old Gobbo (as well as Shylock) the Pantaloon or Senex who opposes the young lovers' desires, Morocco the Captain, and Portia (in the Belmont scenes) Columbine (Mennen, 389). A masque of Pierrots dancing to Bach's Toccata and Fugue in D minor opened the play, while its sets consisted of leaning towers, acutely angled bridges and moving multilevel platforms. This created a crazy, fun-house atmosphere which displaced most of the play's potential seriousness in favor of self-conscious theatricality. Antonio appeared not as the usual pale melancholic but a dandy in flame-colored tights joking with Salerio and Solanio (*Birmingham Gazette*). Their back-slapping rapport later extended to Shylock, who during the first half of the play was performed by Randle Ayrton as a vaudeville comedian. In III.i. the normally dignified and moving "Hath not a Jew eyes" speech was deliberately sent up as Ayrton declaimed it amid thunder-claps and lightning. Yet afterwards in the trial scene he became so coldly repellent that it seemed only fitting to see him outfoxed, even after being spat on by Gratiano (*The Times*). Meanwhile Komisarjevsky poked fun at the fairy-tale unreality of the casket scenes by staging them as waxwork-like displays, with a figurine Portia and attendants appearing on tiered platforms. Eric Lee played Bassanio as an amiable but rather witless fellow who was going to chose the gold casket until Nerissa sang "Tell me where is fancy bred" with exaggerated emphasis on the words rhyming with "lead." Reviewers specially praised Fabia Drake's Portia for being refreshingly believable, especially during the trial scene. Victorian actresses had often treated Portia's lawyer's disguise as a quaint device, using its formal severity as a flattering contrast to their own feminine beauty. Drake, however, appeared genuinely disguised in a wig and large spectacles as a keen young barrister eager to prove himself in his first big case (*The Stage*). Drake was also helped by Komisarjevsky's cut (one of only a few) at III.iv.45-55 where Portia dispatches Balthazar to seek Dr Bellario's legal opinion. The question of when and how Portia finds the loophole in the bond is essential in determining her behavior towards Shylock in the trial and the nature of her character generally. If an audience feels she knows beforehand that she will win, it may seem as if she plays a cat-and-mouse game with Shylock and Antonio to gain attention. Over the years actresses have therefore arrived at different ways of suggesting that Portia does something other than simply borrow Bellario's advice. Drake's Portia, by omitting him, appeared to solve the case herself and so made the trial an assertion of her superior intelligence and authority. This self-sufficiency also countered the impression of passivity in her submission to Bassanio as an obedient wife (III.ii.149ff). Nevertheless these serious implications were always contained within the prevailing comic mood: the Duke snored through the court proceedings while spectators reacted like crowds at a tennis-match. Act V did not therefore come, as so often happens after the terrific tension of IV.i, as an anticlimax, but as a fitting conclusion to the general merriment.

Recent comic productions have taken a more respectful approach to Shakespeare's play, and none has yet to match Komisarjevsky's brilliant originality. Denis Carey's March 1953 production at Stratford-upon-Avon, for instance, was "in the popular tradition" and had exciting moments, yet on the whole left observers dissatisfied because it lacked the edge of moral ambivalence which audiences, since the events of the second world war, now feel performances must convey. Peggy Ashcroft's mature and well-bred Portia established the dominant mood of sophisticated comedy. In I.ii. she felt frustrated with her father's will rather than frivolous tedium: she was more intelligent than to be treated this way, and her response to Shylock reinforced this impression (Cook, 39). Because Carey cut both III.iv. and v, Portia's solution to the bond appeared entirely her own. Ashcroft thought that Portia knew about the loophole as she entered the court but assumed she could convince Shylock to show mercy. But since his express intention is to murder Antonio, in the end she does not act cruelly: "she gives him three chances…and then she strikes" (Cook, 39). Michael Redgrave's Shylock was an absolute contrast to this superior Portia. His "intensely Jewish" Shylock came about after studying Hebrew customs and visiting the Jewish quarter of Amsterdam. Though his thick, wheezing accent disappointed many critics as caricature—Kenneth Tynan described him as "a major prophet with a German accent" (*Evening Standard*)—initially his deliberate pauses in speech conveyed a sense of brooding intelligence and suggested that the idea of revenge formed only gradually; he did not finally resolve to kill Antonio until "Let him look to his bond" at III.i.43. His intellectual powers, however, felt increasingly at odds with his emotional nature as indignation turned into vehement wrath and then into rant (*Birmingham Mail*). Redgrave's outrage grew so excessive during the trial, especially when balanced against Portia's cool restraint, that he may have lost the audience's sympathy, leaving it with impression of a one-dimensional character of total viciousness.

Terry Hands's 1972 Royal Shakespeare Company production achieved similar effects, but set out to do so for different reasons. He tried to let Shakespeare's text speak for itself by giving it, as Martin Esslin observed, "a scrupulously fair, exact rendering: the Jew is a villain, the Gobbos are clowns, the suitors ridiculous, the lovers romantic" (Esslin, 44). As Shylock, Emrys James gratified the Venetians' frequent descriptions of him as a dog by snarling, growling and even barking his lines, thereby dehumanizing the character (*Times*). Susan Fleetwood was passionate but did not balance this with a sense of Portia's high intelligence (*Times*—Dr Bellario was not dropped), or try to harmonize the seemingly contradictory aspects of Portia's personality, from the seemingly spoilt young girl in I.ii. to the sacrificial figure of III.ii. to the commanding lady of V.i. Instead Fleetwood played each scene individually, without suiting her character to modern preferences for realistic psychological development. In short, Hands simply reproduced the text's varied elements without unifying them according to a socially fashionable reading (Esslin, 44), especially those based upon oversympathetic portrayals of Shylock. The production received negative reviews, partly because individual performances were not strong enough to compensate for the play's structural unevenness, but also since its comic approach failed to overturn expectations, now dominant among modern audiences, created by a long tradition of tragic Shylocks.

Tragedy

Nicholas Rowe, compiler of the first critical edition of Shakespeare (1709), was also the first commentator to describe Shylock as tragic, but had in mind Macklin's kind of evil revenger rather than a sympathetic victim. Understanding for Shylock came only towards the end of the eighteenth century under the influence of Romanticism and its typical fascination with heroic outcasts and remote cultures. Although we cannot be sure how widely it was known, Richard Hole's "Apology for the Character and Conduct of Shylock" is characteristic of what was to become the new thinking. Hole asks the reader to put aside prejudices, which are "equally unjust and illiberal," and imagine reversing the play's Jewish and Christian roles. What if Antonio were living in a Jewish society and had been subjected to the same insults as Shylock? Or what if

> a dissipated young Israelite stole an only child from a Christian parent, with a considerable treasure...together with some valuable memorials of former love and friendship? (Hole, 558)

In both cases, Hole argues, we would immediately sympathize with the aggrieved person and not be surprised if he retaliated. Hole's approach is innovative because he treats Shylock as a complex human being whose admittedly evil impulses are not inherently part of his nature but forced upon him by the hostile circumstances of his life. As William Hazlitt later put it:

> The constant apprehension of being burnt alive, plundered, banished, reviled, and trampled on, might be supposed to sour the most forbearing nature, and to take something from that 'milk of human kindness,' with which his persecutors contemplated his indignities. (Characters, 166).

The "problem of Shylock" raised by Romantic essayists also gained validity from a comparison with other plays, since he is just one instance, albeit the most extreme one, of Shakespeare's experiments with outsiders in all his romantic comedies. Like Shylock, Don John in *Much Ado About Nothing*, Jacques in *As You Like It*, and Malvolio in *Twelfth Night* stand apart from society's dominant values and desires. Their exclusion from each play's happy ending darkens its festive mood and defines the limits of dramatic comedy in being able to accommodate all individuals in its drives toward social harmony and self-realization.

What makes Shylock unique, however, is his isolation on religious grounds. As M.M. Mahood explains in the latest Cambridge edition of the play, when Shakespeare came to create the role he turned to Old Testament narratives as sources for Shylock's Jewish character (rather than simply drawing on crude stereotypes as Marlowe had done with Barabbas). Their focal point comes in Shylock's deep identification with Jacob, not only in the story of breeding Laban's sheep (I.iii.70-83) but in the larger theme of Jacob prospering while serving God in an alien society (Genesis 29-35). Shylock's "Laban" speech goes to the heart of his value-system as much as Bassanio's on ornament in III.ii. and Portia's on mercy in IV.i. But because the Old Testament story is now obscure to most audiences, Shylock's morality may seem less rhetorically justified. Jacob's example of "thrift" guides Shylock's business dealings and sustains his self-worth, even though it also marginalizes him among the Christians. For them, on the other hand, merchandising and profit-making is fraught with moral ambivalence. Renaissance custom dictated that "adventuring" in overseas trading was socially acceptable "thrift," whereas taking interest (usury) on loans was not (though it was a common enough practice in the late sixteenth century; Shakespeare himself lent money to neighbors on interest). However, the principle that, ideally, Christians should disavow all "thrift" in keeping with

Jesus' exhortations to poverty still had strong emotional pull in Shakespeare's time, and is reflected in Antonio's pride in lending out money "gratis" to needy borrowers, and in Bassanio's "correct" equation of Portia with lead. The Christians' financial dealings are therefore a continual, and sometimes seemingly hypocritical, compromise with their faith which can make Shylock's forthrightness appear more attractive. Shakespeare makes this point by having Antonio refute Shylock's position with a traditional Christian argument when Antonio is behaving most uncharitably (I.iii.84-129), and allowing Portia's exhortation to mercy to seem contradicted by her vehement insistence that "The Jew shall have all justice."

Shakespeare's suggestions of Shylock's Old Testament heritage as ennobling but in tragic conflict with Christian culture became a key element of romantic productions, beginning with Edmund Kean's in 1814 at Drury Lane. Kean got rid of Shylock's traditional red wig and pointy shoes and was the first to explore the full range of human emotions in his role. Initially he impressed audiences with the dignity and vulnerability of Shylock's religious lineage:

> Shylock is in Venice with his money-bags, his daughter, and his injuries; but his thoughts take wing to the East; his voice swells and deepens at the mention of his sacred tribe and ancient law…(Hawkins, i, 129)

The Venetians by comparison seemed shallow and vain, apt targets of his sharp sarcasm ("Hath a *dog* money? Is it possible / a *cur* can lend three thousand ducats?"). Later in III.i. Kean became agonizingly tormented by Salerio and Solanio's mocking jibes. His agitation reached a climax during the meeting with Tubal, where he alternated convincingly between extreme grief and exultant rage without appearing stagey. This was due partly to Kean's remarkable flexibility of voice, and partly to his overall characterization of Shylock as highly intelligent: in both respects his eloquence surpassed that of any other character (Brown, "Realization," 190-1). Yet Kean was also tender in taking leave of Jessica in II.v. and quietly moving after his defeat. He reacted in mute horror when told he would have to become a Christian and left the court in withering contempt for the proceedings. The sight of this proud-spirited man being crushed struck audiences as overwhelmingly pitiful.

Henry Irving's performances later in the century extended Kean's reading in a different direction. "Shylock" he explained, "is a bloody-minded monster,—but you mustn't play him so if you wish to succeed; you must get some sympathy with him" (Winter, *Shakespeare*, 175). Whereas Kean made Shylock a symbol of his ancient race, Irving's figure was an individual Jew whose stately and sober personality was provoked into a cold fury by the Venetians' doubledealings, but ultimately demolished. Irving's 1879 production at the Lyceum ran for over 250 nights, during which time his Shylock gradually became more ruthless, though always tragic.

One detail epitomizing Irving's approach was the scene he added at the end of II.vi. after Lorenzo steals away with Jessica. Lines 60-8 were cut ("No masque tonight, the wind is come about") and replaced with a Carnival tableau of masquers dancing to pipes, tabors, and "jangling bells." As the festivity moved off, the curtain fell and then quickly rose again to reveal Shylock looking scornfully in the direction of the music and going to the door of his darkened house; he knocked twice, there was a long silence, and the curtain again dropped. Ellen Terry, playing Portia, recalled that

> For absolute pathos, achieved by absolute simplicity of means, I never saw anything in the theatre to compare with his [Irving's] Shylock's return home over the bridge to his deserted house after Jessica's flight. (Story, 186)

In his next scene, III.i, where Shylock is usually played with stormy emotion, Irving stood quietly seething in the face of Salerio and Solanio's insults (Winter, *Shakespeare*, 187-8). Only after Tubal arrived did his composure shatter, his breakdown conveying the sense of a whole world of feeling, normally kept tightly in reserve, finally overcharged by unbearable grief. Irving rallied at "I will have the *heart* of him if he forfeit" (120), signalling his determination to kill Antonio. But afterwards he again broke down, tearing open his robes and beating his breast in Job-like lamentation.

Irving repeated this emotional pattern during the trial, which reviewers considered to be the high point of his performance. Until the bond's reversal, it was as if the wounds of III.i. had been cauterized: Irving's gestures were cold and unshakeably focused; he had "the horrible stillness and fascination of the rattle-snake" (Lelyveld, 88). Then after Portia's coup this steely control gave way in a

> total collapse of mind and body, when at a glance the full significance of the words—'This bond doth give thee here no jot of blood'—burst upon his keen intellect. In these words, and what follows, he seems to receive his death-blow. (Brown, "Realization," 194-5)

When leaving the court Shylock temporarily recovered, drawing himself to his full height and sneering defiantly at Gratiano's braying insults. But at the exit he collapsed again and slowly dragged himself away to utter three anguished yells off-stage.

Besides Irving's Shylock, Victorian audiences thronged the Lyceum to see the magnificent scenery and Ellen Terry's Portia. In keeping with the century's taste for visual display, Irving's production featured large picture-postcard backdrops of Venice and Belmont and finely detailed costumes. Gondolas meandering along canals, fruit and water-carriers, and Oriental lanterns all gratified playgoers' appetites for "local color." Irving also filled the courtroom with a huge gallery of spectators who dutifully hissed and jeered Shylock, thereby heightening the audience's feelings of compassion for the underdog. Such massed and sumptuous effects were only achieved, however, by freely adapting Shakespeare's text. Besides the added scene discussed above, scenes II.ix. and III.v. (Aragon; Jessica, Launcelot and Lorenzo) were cut along with much of Act V (Irving initially deleted the entire scene but later restored part of it).

Portia's dialogue with Nerissa in I.ii. and elsewhere was also reduced, as was much of the poetry in III.ii. In such circumstances, it is surprising that Ellen Terry managed to make anything of the role whatsoever; but then again many members of the audience obviously came more for the actress than for Portia. Originally Terry conceived her personality as quiet and modest. But when Irving decided to play a reserved Shylock, Terry felt she had to be more outgoing, portraying an exquisitely refined woman—"La Serenissima," the embodiment of legendary Venice: "Portia is the fruit of the Renaissance, the child of the period of beautiful clothes, beautiful cities, beautiful houses, beautiful ideas" (*Four Lectures,* 119). At the same time Terry was wary of appearing too "lady-fied" and tried to project Portia's independence. Passages in I.ii. referring to her irrationality (16-18) and submission to her father's will (19-24, 88-90) were cut to make it appear she was in greater control of her own destiny. Terry also refused to be coy about her affections for Bassanio, seeing no point in behaving "like a Victorian maiden" *(Story*, 184). Some reviewers, however, felt that this carried independence too far: "Miss Terry's mistress of Belmont giggles too much, plays too much with her fingers, is too free and familiar, too osculatory in her relations with Bassanio," said Henry James (*Scenic Art*, 143). But Terry presumably consoled herself that the same reviewers found her "sweet self-surrender" to Bassanio as "her lord, her governor, her king" highly satisfactory.

Terry recognized some of the potential contradictions in Portia's role but decided not to smooth them out too much. Her approach was entirely different from that of the notable Portia of the previous generation, Helen Faucit, who played opposite early Victorian Shylocks such as Charles Macready and Charles Kemble. Whereas Terry's informing trait was beauty, Faucit's was disciplined intelligence combined with obedience to her father's will (Faucit, 30-1). This more earnest reading suited some scenes better than others. In the early ones Faucit's humor at the expense of her suitors lacked the guilelessness conveyed by Terry's carefree gaiety (Foulkes, "*Faucit and Terry*," 29). But Faucit was more successful than Terry in facing Shylock. She believed that Portia was intelligent enough to find the loophole herself before leaving Belmont, and that Bellario simply provided the legal confirmation. This had the advantage of making Portia's otherwise strangely jolly mood as she sets out with Nerissa for Venice (III.iv.57ff) seem convincing. Like all actresses who do not take Faucit's decision (or something like it), Terry had difficulty making this interlude work; to one observer it appeared "a girlish freak" (Foulkes, "*Faucit and Terry*," 31). Faucit's approach served her equally well at the trial: her genuine disguise as a confident young lawyer seemed like the natural outcome of the personality Faucit had been preparing the audience for in previous scenes, and allowed her to be forceful in appealing to Shylock. Having given him several chances to relent, however, Faucit's heart became "almost as stony as his own" (a reaction similar to Peggy Ashcroft's), though she speculated later that Portia would not approve of Antonio's harsh conditions.

Ellen Terry did not come to Venice with any preconceived solution nor did she encourage spectators' suspension of disbelief in Portia's disguise, which she viewed as a thin dramatic convention. Instead she entered the court "'radiant in her rose-coloured lawyer's gown, with her face wreathed in smiles'" (Hicks, 51), relying ultimately on the audience's knowledge that such situations always turn out well in the end. She tried various ways of dissuading Shylock until suddenly she had a flash of inspiration: "Tarry a little, there is something else" (300). Terry later admitted that this reading left Portia too little time before line 309, "Thyself shalt see the act" (Bandel, 50). Yet like Faucit she too had doubts about the severity of Shylock's punishment. In her published memoirs Terry defended her performance claiming "desperate evils demand desperate remedies;" but in her original manuscript, subsequently altered by her publisher, she confessed that the Christians' behavior "has an unattractive element of moral deceit—of the dangerous doctrine that the means is justified by the end" (Bandel, 48). In all events these scruples did not deter her from swiftly reverting to high comedy after the trial and in the abbreviated final scene—a welcome relief after the tension of Irving's drawn-out exit. Faucit on the other hand kept her disguise on in the last act and balanced its comedy with some serious scolding of Bassanio for his broken vows, thus stressing Portia's high-minded personality to the end.

To return to Irving's production overall, although it was undoubtedly original it nonetheless distorted the play by concentrating disproportionately on Shylock and disrupting Shakespeare's careful alternation between Venice and Belmont in favor of isolated "big" scenes (though this was typical of many nineteenth-century productions). To critics, the result was not Shakespeare at all but what Shaw derided as "the Martyrdom of Irving." Since then directors have reinstated more of Shakespeare's text, while presenting its themes of money and anti-semitism and its characters more realistically. In particular, the immediacy of twentieth-century persecution has led tragic productions to present Shylock's story as as a case-study in oppression. The Christians' hypocrisy is magnified and their intolerance of outsiders extended to Jessica, whom comic productions portray as glad to join Christian society, and to Antonio, whose affection for Bassanio and lack of a marriage partner is taken to imply latent or even open homosexuality. Under such conditions the play's romantic comedy has never been harder to present in anything like an innocent or straightforward way.

All these traits characterized Jonathan Miller's May 1970 National Theatre production with Sir Laurence Olivier as Shylock and Joan Plowright as Portia. Miller's highly detailed late-nineteenth-century setting conveyed an atmosphere of material opulence and psychological realism familiar from Victorian novels (Berry, 32). Antonio and Shylock appeared almost identically dressed in top-hats, frock coats and pin-striped trousers, members of a privileged stockbroker-world. Olivier was sober and refined, his proposal of the "merry bond" being a sophisticated jest intended to ingratiate himself with his business associates. But small things such as the discrete skull-cap underneath his hat and a voice straining to imitate the upper-class accents around him indicated that he didn't quite belong (*Guardian*). Miller sought to limit the audience's resistance to Shylock by cutting the opening aside "I hate him for he is a Christian," and making it plain that his fussy mannerisms were the result of trying to become accepted by "gentle" society.

Olivier also gained considerable sympathy by contrast with the Christians. Luxurious living had sapped them of any spontaneous feelings, with the exception of Antonio's frustrated devotion to Bassanio; his normally revealing lines at I.i.120-2 ("tell me now what lady is the same") were reduced to a curt "Well?" (*Times*). Bassanio was interested in Portia only because she was "richly left," while she was looking for anybody who could divert her boredom. Critics described her as smug and "bossy" during the casket scenes, which Miller burlesqued as sentimental nonsense (Portia's submission speech, "You see me, Lord Bassanio, where I stand," became flat parody). While treating all social inferiors with slight contempt, Portia was openly condescending towards Jessica, whose name she kept forgetting after her arrival with Lorenzo in Belmont.

Jessica's flight finally exploded Shylock's careful efforts at becoming assimilated into Christian society. In III.i. Olivier faced the same difficulty as all actors playing Shylock, since the text requires him to enter in distraction but without any transition to ensure the emotional change is convincing. Miller dealt with this problem by having Olivier first overhear Salerio and Solanio from a balcony and then descend to them in a fury. Instead of delivering "Hath not a Jew eyes" for pathos, Olivier made it a taunting justification for his revenge (Foulkes, "*Irving and Olivier*," 33).

Later in the Tubal scene, Olivier balanced Shylock's deep grief with elation at the news of Antonio's losses, at one point doing a little victory dance, which reminded some reviewers, ironically, of Hitler's dance of triumph at the fall of Paris. This was also the moment his suppressed ancestry resurfaced, as Olivier solemnly wrapped himself in a prayer scarf to join Tubal at their synagogue. During IV.i. Olivier resembled Irving in behaving with quiet but deadly resolve, although Miller's setting was very different: instead of a crowded public court, Shylock encountered Portia over a massive table in a private boardroom. Olivier also dealt ingeniously with the problem of Shylock appearing bloodthirsty when he sharpens his knife during the proceedings by having a servant do the job instead (Foulkes, "*Irving and Olivier*," 33). After Portia reversed the bond Olivier was incredulous ("Is *that* the law?) and then seemed to physically implode. In facing the Duke's sentence and Gratiano's gloating taunts (delivered in between swigs from a hip-flask), Shylock had to be supported under both arms but eventually gathered enough strength to depart with controlled dignity. It was then that Olivier's performance most recalled Irving's, for offstage he gave a long, unforgettable howl of pain, which the shift of action to Belmont could do little to dispel. Portia was glum on returning home, and both she and Nerissa baited Bassanio and Gratiano aggressively about the rings. At the end Antonio and Jessica were left alone onstage reading the letters Portia had distributed before tripping off with the others. The return of Antonio's ships failed to compensate for the loss of his foremost place in Bassanio's affections, while a Jewish song of mourning rose in the background and Jessica's face suggested that though she was now one of "them," she was destined to share her father's fate as a perpetual outsider (*Observer*).

Though Miller's production left very little comedy intact, even less survived in Bill Alexander's for the RSC in May 1987, which presented the most brutal and uncompromising version of the play yet staged. Against a bare brick wall scrawled with anti-semitic graffiti and amidst freaks darting in and out, Salerio and Solanio entered over a bridge spitting viciously at Tubal underneath, and shouting "Jew, Jew!" as he ran away. From this fierce opening onwards, Alexander continually confronted the audience with acts and symbols of persecution, such as the yellow star Shylock wore during the trial. Antony Sher played him as an aggressive gypsy merchandiser, the antithesis of Olivier's refined and assimilated Jew, who gained the audience's compassion not through any sympathetic traits of his own, but owing to Christian abuse. Alexander cut Shylock's passages about dreaming of moneybags and ending Antonio's business interference (II.v.19; III.i.104-6) to remove avarice and mercantile rivalry as motives for revenge in favor of racial hatred alone. Sher's single-mindedness in this respect even overrode grief for Shylock's family losses in III.i. He entered the scene bleeding from his forehead and being stoned by a crowd of children who had picked up the chant "Jew, Jew!" After being reviled by Salerio and Solanio, Sher delivered "Hath not a Jew eyes" quietly so that he could work up to an explosion at "The villainy you teach me I will execute" (59-60), which proved to be the key to his interpretation (*Spectator*). And the Christians *had* taught Shylock well. All were spitting Jew-baiters except for John Carlisle's Antonio, sunk in gloom at the prospect of losing Bassanio, whom he kissed passionately at the end of I.i and iii. Antonio was so besotted that he remained unperturbed by Shylock during the trial and openly welcomed death as a release from his wretched existence (*Guardian*).

The Belmont scenes provided no relief to these tensions. Deborah Findlay's Portia was spoilt and arrogant, indulging in nasty little racial jokes in I.ii, openly disdaining Morocco's skin-color in II.vii. ("Let all of his complexion choose me so"), and laughing at Aragon when he chose the wrong casket. There was no love between Portia and Bassanio, only relief on her part that the parade of unspeakable men would end, and glee on his at hitting the jackpot. Portia's behavior, like everybody else's, was learnt from her hostile surroundings. As Irving Wardle suggested in *The Times*, she had been subjected for years to men's impositions and now took any opportunity available to respond with deeds of feminist cruelty. Shylock became her target in IV.i. (thus rendering the "quality of mercy" speech insincere) and Bassanio a more deserving one during the unusually prickly ring episode. Like Miller's production, Alexander's final act extended the tension of IV.i. rather than countering it with comedy. He reversed the order of Antonio's conditions at the trial's climax by having Shylock's conversion to Christianity (IV.i.381) follow the deed of gift to Lorenzo and Jessica (IV.i.382-4). Bassanio and Gratiano immediately gripped Shylock in an armlock and forced him to kneel and cross himself. In the play's final moment Antonio was left alone with Jessica on stage and offered her the crucifix she had dropped, perhaps deliberately, after the others had retired inside.

Although Sher's terrific energy and the evocative symbolism of Alexander's production made for exciting theatre, it was equally obvious that this was not "the Jew that Shakespeare drew." All the text's potential ambivalence, as well as its romantic lyricism, had been dislocated by the single idea of racial warfare. And though Shylock was notoriously abused, he had been deformed too. For Alexander it was clear that the play's comic premises—the Christians' strained principles of love and benevolence—were simply no longer viable in a post-Holocaust world. Yet if this were now the only possible view of the play a more honest approach would be never to stage it again, since without the ideals represented (however deficiently) by Belmont, the play is no longer Shakespeare's. Other directors, however, have refused to allow the play's racial conflict to become its sole concern. Since it is hard to imagine anybody going much further than Alexander (short of rewriting the play, as Arnold Wesker and Charles Marowitz have done), and since comic productions which deny sympathy for Shylock's anger have become unacceptable since the second World War, some recent directors have sought an alternative to the two established traditions of performance. They hope to avoid the sentimentality and narrowness of "tragic" Shylocks while granting more scope for audience discomfort than comic productions normally allow. The anti-semitism of Shylock's adversaries is openly acknowledged, but not at the cost of condemning everything the Christians represent. Greater dramatic attention is also paid to Portia's situation as a woman constrained by the laws of a man's world. In short, these directors see their task as letting the play's multiple and often irreconcilable actions develop freely, rather than subjecting them to one dominant viewpoint. This means blurring the differences between Jew and Christian to break down the cultural solitudes which invite audiences to take sides, and also highlighting certain verbal and thematic features which cut both ways, from Gratiano's simple echo at IV.i.328 of Shylock's vengeful "If I can catch him once upon the hip" (I.iii.39), to the lack of self-evident moral superiority in Antonio's way of doing business over Shylock's. The result is a composite approach which foregrounds the play's coexistent tragic and comic features, thereby creating an atmosphere of moral relativism.

This new perspective does not necessarily represent a more definitive or even more desirable reading of the play. But it has added a fresh dimension to *The Merchant's* stage-life, and decisively influenced the views of recent critics.

"Mixed Comedy"

One of the most frequent remarks made by reviewers of Michael Langham's May 1960 production at Stratford-upon-Avon concerned its quick pace and dance-like stage movement. Episodes in Venice and Belmont revolved with close juxtapositions of their confrontational and happy moments, each evoked with vigor and depth. Although not all critics liked his treatment of the play, Langham's point seemed to be that, as in music, the play's final harmony could only seem genuine if it were preceded by a lively interplay of dramatic dissonances. Thus his production did not shy away from clashes in mood caused by Shakespeare's generically mixed actions, but which predominantly tragic or comic performances try to soften according to their preferred viewpoint. The fast clip also encouraged audiences not to settle into one pattern of theatrical response but remain alert to the play's diversity.

Elegant eighteenth-century costumes and bright sets established the production's major key centered in Belmont, while Venice was contrastingly sombre. Langham divided attention fairly equally among Antonio, Shylock and Portia. The former, played by Patrick Allen, was an intensely anguished figure suffering from a deep but physically restrained attraction to Denholm Elliot's Bassanio (*Birmingham Post*). Antonio's isolation in the midst of many friends suggested parallels with Shylock: both were temperamentally reserved men whose craving for emotional security, from Bassanio and Jessica respectively, was a byproduct of their high-profile commercial activities. When Antonio was left on stage at the end of the play repossessed of "life and living" but lacking joy in either, his bereavement recalled Shylock's hollow "I am content" at the end of the trial. Peter O'Toole's Shylock was not a racial symbol, even though he spoke in clipped snatches with a heavy Yiddish accent. Rather he played a virile and witty individualist who was equally proud and vindictive. He bore the pain of

Venetian insults, and later of Jessica's betrayal, with heroic self-control, only yielding very late to a monumental urge for revenge. His true antithesis was Portia, played by Dorothy Tutin. In the early scenes she was fresh and outgoing, leaving the audience in no doubts about why Bassanio was enamoured with her (*Times*). But her greatest achievement was being able to suggest convincingly Portia's emotional growth and intellectual maturation from I.ii. onward. In III.ii., as Robert Speaight recalled, "you saw a girl suddenly transformed" by love into an ardent woman, who then became serious and authoritative in responding to Antonio's danger, and successfully carried over this mood into IV.i. As a result, Portia's lighter moment with Nerissa before leaving for Venice did not seem like misplaced frivolity but a way of temporarily relieving anxiety about the trial's outcome. As Antonio's advocate she firmly matched Shylock's determination yet was sincere in her belief in mercy, which she confirmed after the reversal by rebuking a taunting crowd which had formed around Shylock, and raising him from his knees to allow him a dignified departure. Afterwards Langham strongly emphasised the poetic lyricism and sexual playfulness of the last act. As elsewhere in his production, these shifts in mood came swiftly and without apology, with most reviewers feeling that unease over Shylock did not linger to spoil the final comedy. Although several felt the production failed to jell, Langham seemed to be more interested in "pointing the form of the play, its crises, contrasts, repetitions, developments" and ensuring "that the audience was involved in the play as a whole" (Brown, "*Three Directors*," 136).

Instead of encouraging playgoers to revel in *The Merchant's* various moods, John Barton in 1978 asked them to analyze it according to a single theme: true versus false value in human relationships (Barton, 169-70). All the main characters were intensely realistic, with carefully considered stage details creating full psychological portraits. Barton's RSC production at The Other Place in Stratford-upon-Avon was sparsely set in late nineteenth-century Italy and, as many reviewers observed, carried an air of melancholy until the brighter last act. In I.ii. Nerissa had to prompt a timid Portia (Marjorie Bland), still mourning the death of her father, to cheer herself up by poking fun at her suitors. Later Portia faced alarming prospects in Morocco, who kept pawing her during his speeches, and Aragon, a slick proto-fascist (Overton, 59-61). Increasingly the casket-game seemed like a trap which she and her household needed desperately to escape, so that by III.ii. the tension before Bassanio's choice became "electric" (Warren, 204).

Barton's concentration on Portia's ordeal ensured that for once she was not overshadowed by Shylock. Patrick Stewart presented a deliberately low-key figure who was not a racial symbol but "a bad human and a bad Jew" (*Brockbank, Players*, 19). He brilliantly captured Shylock's meanness by carrying around a tin in which he carefully saved cigarette stubs for reuse. Stewart believed that Shylock's obsession with material security had taught him to cut all emotional ties by putting up a "protective smoke-screen" of comic banter to appease the self-centered Christians and insulate himself from their abuses. This detachment extended equally to Launcelot and Jessica, and at one point Stewart shocked audiences by giving her a slap on the face. Shylock's alienation even from the Jewish community became apparent in III.i. when Tubal, whose smart clothes contrasted sharply with Shylock's shabby gabardine, became strongly disapproving when Stewart showed far more grief for the loss of his ducats than his daughter. Shylock's decision to kill Antonio came coldly at the end of the scene, where an emphasis on "were he out of Venice I can make what merchandise I will" (120-1) indicated that his motives were still mainly commercial (Warren, 205). During the trial Stewart was almost casually restrained, plucking aside a black servant to justify the argument "You have among you many a purchased slave," but otherwise remaining calm except when Portia briefly appeared to side with him. When the tables turned, Shylock shrugged off the defeat by humbling himself before the Duke, shaking hands with Antonio, and even laughing at Gratiano's mockery; all this was Shylock's pragmatic reversion to playing the "eccentric clown" to ensure that, as always, he survived (*Brockbank, Players*, 27). Stewart's striking but unheroic performance prevented the fifth act from seeming like a wrenching shift and allowed the Christians to celebrate their winning fortunes with genuine humor. Overall, Barton's production clarified the familiar pattern of Shakespearian comedy whereby the protagonists pass from death and mourning to growth and renewal, without denying *The Merchant's* special emphasis on the human suffering that can attend that process.

Nonetheless his production was also highly unusual in virtually ignoring the play's religious conflict. Patrick Stewart considered Shylock to be an outsider who happens also to be an untypical Jew. But when the production transferred to London and David Suchet took over the role he re-established anti-semitism as a chief concern: Shylock is an outsider because he is Jewish (Barton, 170-1). This view was shared by Sir Peter Hall's June 1989 production, which tried like Barton's to make the play's characters and conflicts as psychologically complex as possible. His set—a series of Italian Renaissance colonades—remained in place throughout the play and so suggested that Belmont and Venice were identical. Shylock's presence failed to disrupt their overlapping atmospheres because, more than Patrick Stewart, Dustin Hoffman portrayed him as an unsentimental and self-effacing Jew. Hoffman's small stature and humble manner created the impression of an "ordinary little guy" who survived by keeping his resentment concealed behind a conciliatory social mask (*Jewish Chronicle*). His Shylock went out of his way to avoid giving offense, calmly wiping Antonio's spittle off his clothes and deliberately smiling through his own angry lines in I.iii. This exceptional forbearance also delayed his decision to take revenge until late in III.i. There Shylock's chief sense of loss at the news of Jessica's betrayal was personal, since earlier in II.v. he had parted lovingly from her, thus causing her great anxiety in making the decision to steal away (*Times*). During the trial scene, however, Hoffman reverted to his small-scale manner and therefore was easily crushed by Geraldine James's no-nonsense Portia. He expressed no resentment and generated no pathos in being "bundled off" and soon was easily forgotten.

The point of Shylock's quietism became clear within the larger context of the Christians' behavior. Although they slighted Shylock continually, they did so unthinkingly, not in the vicious manner of Alexander's Jew-baiters. Their commercial double standards were readily apparent but not stressed. Antonio's affection for Bassanio was genuine and moving, and its homosexual nature was only hinted at. Bassanio was charming, not over-confident, and honestly aware of his self-interest in journeying to Belmont (*Daily Telegraph*). James played Portia consistently as a mature, serious woman (lacking humor and a bit thick, according to some critics), who was true to her own instincts even if they occasionally trampled on the feelings of others (*N.Y. Times*). On the whole, then, Hall did not present a gallery of wicked Christians meant to sting the audience's conscience; though they were intolerant towards aliens such as Shylock and Morocco, amongst themselves they were sincere and agreeable (*Sunday Times*). This apparently relaxed attitude towards the play's anti-semitism carried an implicit ability to mirror the audience's own "soft" responses. One effect of the Venetians' casual spitting was that after a while one could get used to it and thus become in danger of reacting as indifferently to Shylock's scorned humanity as the Venetians themselves. Hall made a similar point by transposing Salerio and Solanio's description of Shylock in II.viii. to the beginning of III.i. As David Nathan reported the two "Salads" tried to be funny by mimicking Shylock's laments in comic stage-Yiddish accents. But as soon as Shylock entered they spat on him, indicating the potential venom in such "harmless" ethnic jokes for the outsider. These moments were brief, however, and on the whole the Christians' faults, as Shakespeare's text itself suggests, remained implicit rather than being dissected openly. For most spectators, Hall's production was enjoyable because the Christians' aspirations and theirs coalesced with few areas of disagreement.

By highlighting this condition of moral amnesia, "mixed comedy" productions of course reflect the fashionable skepticism of late twentieth-century audiences, and therefore continue the tendency of virtually every production since the eighteenth century to mirror contemporary opinions on race and religion. They likewise present the Christians' actions as typical of the way all dominant social groups make peace with injustice while believing themselves to act according to higher codes of behavior. The moral touchstone for this situation has become Portia, now rescued from her largely ornamental past; for when her part—the longest in the play—is given full scope she is most capable of becoming aware of the persistent gap between Christian principle and action, yet equally aware that such recognition does not necessarily translate into better conduct. In exploring the consequences of this pessimistic conclusion, recent productions have paired Shylock and Antonio's final reactions ("I am content" / "I am dumb") to suggest that perhaps an individual's only proper response is radical humility. This would anticipate the reactions of Parolles (under humorous circumstances) in *All's Well That Ends Well*, and Lear (belatedly, under earth-shattering ones), and therefore support what many critics see as the strong affinities between *The Merchant of Venice* and Shakespeare's later problem comedies and tragedies. But thematically and structurally *The Merchant* remains a romantic comedy, and in this context the strong emphasis of recent productions on human self-deception and universal moral culpability in the play may seem distorting. Audiences may still wish to see Shakespeare's humanitarianism being given a fighting chance against his self-created odds, and not to dismiss absolutely Lorenzo's vision of celestial concord affirming compassion and benevolence as sustainable community ideals, however much this "muddy vesture of decay" keeps them from ever becoming fully realized.

Date

Although a precise date for the play's composition cannot be established, it is thought to fall within the period between autumn 1596 and summer 1598. The earlier limit is provided by the apparent allusion at I.i.27 to the St Andrew, a Spanish galleon taken by the English at Cadiz in 1596. Its capture was first reported in August 1596, and remained in the news that autumn. The play cannot have been written later than 22 July 1598 when it was entered in the Stationers' Register. In the same year on 7 September Francis Meres mentioned it in *Palladis Tamia*.

Fuller discussion of the play's dating and of its textual history can be found in the editions by Brown and Mahood listed in the Bibliography.

INTRODUCTION NOTES

[1]Marginal note on Booth at I.iii.29 in Castle Square Theatre promptbook of *The Merchant of Venice* (dir. Winthrop Ames, c. 1920s), New York Public Library.

CHARACTERS

THE DUKE OF VENICE

ANTONIO, a merchant

SHYLOCK, a Jewish merchant

JESSICA, his daughter

BASSANIO, Antonio's friend, suitor to Portia

GRATIANO, Antonio's and Bassanio's friend

LORENZO, in love with Jessica

TUBAL, Shylock's friend

SALERIO, Antonio's and Bassanio's friend

SOLANIO, Antonio's and Bassanio's friend

LEONARDO, Bassanio's servant

LAUNCELOT GOBBO, a clown, Shylock's servant, and later Bassanio's servant

GOBBO, old father of Launcelot

SERVINGMAN of Antonio

PORTIA, an heiress of Belmont

NERISSA, her companion and waiting-woman

THE PRINCE OF MOROCCO, suitor to Portia

THE PRINCE OF ARAGON, suitor to Portia

BALTHAZAR, Portia's servant

STEPHANO, Portia's servant

MAGNIFICOS of VENICE, JAILER, OFFICERS of the COURT, SERVANTS, ATTENDANTS, MUSICIANS.

ACT I

Scene i Enter ANTONIO, SALERIO, and SOLANIO.

ANTONIO In sooth° I know not why I am so sad,
It wearies me, you say it wearies you;
But how I caught it, found it, or came by it,
What stuff 'tis made of, whereof it is born,
I am° to learn;°
And such a want-wit° sadness makes of me
That I have much ado to know myself.

SALERIO Your mind is tossing on the ocean,
There where your argosies° with portly° sail
Like signors° and rich burghers° on the flood,
Or as it were the pageants° of the sea,
Do overpeer° the petty traffickers
That curtsy to them, do them reverence
As they° fly by them with their woven wings.

SOLANIO Believe me, sir, had I such venture° forth,
The better part of my affections° would
Be with my hopes abroad. I should be still°
Plucking° the grass to know where sits the wind°,
Peering in maps for ports and piers and roads°,
And every object° that might make me fear
Misfortune to my ventures, out of° doubt
Would make me sad.

SALERIO My wind cooling my broth
Would blow° me to an ague° when I thought
What harm a wind too great might do at sea.
I should not see the sandy hourglass run
But I should think of shallows and of flats,°
And see my wealthy Andrew° docked in sand,

ACT I. Scene i

truth

have yet find out

one lacking understanding

large merchant ships full and majestic

distinguished gentlemen citizens

festive barges or floats

look down upon

i.e: the argosies

risky enterprise at sea

feelings and thoughts

always

i.e. tossing in the air i.e. its on coming direction

open harbors

mishap

no

excite shivering fever

shoals

Spanish galleon captured in 1596

1-7 The play begins in mid-conversation and at an emotional highpoint. Are the characters going to a specific place on stage? or is their intention to walk across, while one or the other keeps holding them back? or do they stop walking because of the emotional pitch of the conversation? In some productions all three are 'discovered' on stage.

Is Antonio glad of Salerio's and Solanio's company? Is he courteously suffering their presence or would he like to be alone? Line 5 suggests six syllables of silence within the iambic pentameter. Why has Antonio run out of words? Is he incapable of talking about his emotions? Is it self-deprecating humour? Does he know what is wrong but does not find Salerio and Solanio sufficiently intimate friends? There is the opportunity to change the rhythm of the speech with the last two lines: might it wind down the conversation? or does it invite Salerio's and Solanio's support. Either way, Antonio falls silent for the next 32 lines.

8-14 Salerio's speech has to have the feeling of being improvised and developed as he goes along. Is he trying to get Antonio out of his mood? but not easily at home with this language? The speech loses drive at lines 11 and 13. These rhythmic shifts can underpin the improvisatory quality of the speech: Salerio might be looking at Antonio and falter because he is not getting through?

15-20 Solanio takes over: does he want to be the person who changes Antonio's mood, or is the audience supposed to think Salerio and Solanio are a double act? Perhaps Antonio's silence is so unusual, resolute or desperate, that both feel a need to fill it at any price. With 'sir', an audience understands that Antonio is the more powerful figure: they may be friends, but they are not intimates.

21-40 Line 22 is shared between Solanio and Salerio. Is there recognition by Solanio (or both of

Vailing° her high top° lower than her ribs
To kiss her burial.° Should I go to church
And see the holy edifice of stone
And not bethink° me straight of dangerous rocks,
Which touching but my gentle° vessel's side
Would scatter all her spices on the stream,
Enrobe the roaring waters with my silks,
And, in a word, but even now worth this°
And now° worth nothing? Shall I have the thought
To think on this, and shall I lack the thought
That such a thing bechanced° would make me sad?
But tell not me; I know Antonio
Is sad to think upon his merchandise.

ANTONIO Believe me, no. I thank my fortune for it,
My ventures are not in one bottom° trusted
Nor to one place, nor is my whole estate
Upon° the fortune of this present year.
Therefore my merchandise makes me not sad.

SOLANIO Why then you are in love.

ANTONIO Fie, fie.

SOLANIO Not in love neither? Then let us say you are sad
Because you are not merry, and 'twere as easy
For you to laugh and leap and say you are merry
Because you are not sad. Now by two-headed Janus,°
Nature hath framed strange fellows in her time:
Some that will evermore peep through their eyes°
And laugh like parrots° at a bagpiper,°
And other of such vinegar° aspect
That they'll not show their teeth in way of smile
Though° Nestor° swear the jest be laughable.

Enter BASSANIO, LORENZO, and GRATIANO.

Here comes Bassanio your most noble kinsman,
Gratiano, and Lorenzo. Fare ye well,
We leave you now with better company.

SALERIO I would have stayed till I had made you merry,
If worthier friends had not prevented° me.

lowering, bowing topsail
burial ground

think straight away
delicate, noble

in one moment worth ever-thing
suddenly

if it happened

ship's hold committed

dependent on

Roman god with two faces, one sad, one merry
because half-closed by laughter
proverbially foolish i.e. "gloomy" music
sour
even though oldest and most dignified Greek leader in the Trojan wars

anticipated

them) that his strategy, too, is not working? or, is Salerio thinking they are beginning to have some effect?

Where Solanio's speech was more direct and in keeping with Antonio's, Salerio's is now rhythmically more assured. 'Antonio' in line 39 is the first time a character is named, and the direct address compels him to respond. Do all three sense their speeches have gone on too long?

41-45 Antonio says his merchandise does not make him sad and is not trusted to one ship, nor one place, nor is all his money in these ventures. But later (1.1.178-179) he will say to Bassanio that all his fortunes are at sea, he has neither money nor commodity. To whom is Antonio telling the truth? Does he wish to stop Salerio's and Solanio's conversation? is he telling the truth to them but lying to Bassanio; or is he simply careless about his business details?

46-57 Lines 46 and 47 are short lines. Does Solanio understand from Antonio's 'Fie, fie' in conjunction with his silence that Antonio might be in love? Solanio carries the conversation forward. His tone is more forthright. Does he accept Antonio's reaction at face value, and gives up trying to understand his sadness? or does he accept that Antonio is not in love but uses irony and sarcasm to badger him into new humour? or does he believe Antonio is in love and uses irony to try getting through to him? or is he in love with Antonio himself? Antonio again falls silent. In Solanio's speech the images become more exaggerated and less clustered into coherent groups (eg ships, sea), he is working harder and becoming verbally wilder, which highlights Antonio's silence all the more.

58-69 It is almost a relief when Bassanio, Lorenzo and Gratiano enter. Solanio and Salerio quickly bid Antonio farewell. Do they see Antonio's reaction to the groups approach? Antonio is courteous but makes no effort to stop Salerio and Solanio from going. He falls back into silence.

ANTONIO Your worth is very dear in my regard.
I take it your own business calls on you,
And you embrace th'occasion° to depart.

SALERIO Good morrow my good lords.

BASSANIO Good signors both, when shall we laugh?° Say, when?
You grow exceeding strange;° must it be so?

SALERIO We'll make our leisures to attend on° yours.

Exeunt SALERIO and SOLANIO.

LORENZO My lord Bassanio, since you have found Antonio,
We two will leave you; but at dinnertime
I pray you have in mind where we must meet.

BASSANIO I will not fail you.

GRATIANO You look not well, Signor Antonio.
You have too much respect upon the world;°
They lose it that do buy it with much care.
Believe me, you are marvellously° changed.

ANTONIO I hold the world but as the world, Gratanio,
A stage where every man must play a part,
And mine a sad one.

GRATIANO Let me play the fool!
With mirth and laughter let old wrinkles come,
And let my liver° rather heat with wine
Than my heart cool° with mortifying° groans.
Why should a man whose blood is warm within
Sit like his grandsire cut in alabaster?°
Sleep when he wakes? And creep into the jaundice
By being peevish?° I tell thee what, Antonio,
I love thee, and 'tis my love that speaks:
There are a sort of men whose visages
Do cream and mantle° like a standing° pond,
And do a wilful stillness entertain,°
With purpose to be dressed in an opinion°
Of wisdom, gravity, profound conceit,°
As who should say,° "I am Sir Oracle,°
And when I ope my lips, let no dog bark."°

opportunity

be merry together

distant

fit in with

70-77 Line 73 is a short line, and Bassanio's silent beats may point to his being distracted, or just looking at Antonio, or lost in his thoughts. Does he wonder how to begin a conversation? Is Lorenzo trying to exit in this, urging Gratiano to come along?

Gratino stays—his first line suggesting that he has not seen Antonio for some time and is struck by the change in him: he is 'unwell', he is 'marvellously chang'd'. Gratiano's observation agrees with Salerio and Solanio; and like them, Gratiano too assumes he has changed because of his business.

concern for worldly business

astonishingly

78-81 Antonio addresses Gratiano by name, suggesting he is closer than Salerio and Solanio. Does Antonio's reply suggest he is alienated from himself? Is he watching himself in this condition? Might Antonio point the line at Bassanio?

Has Antonio finished his speech, or does Gratiano interrupt him? Gratianio picks up on the world as a stage by wanting to play Antonio's fool. In line 77 he again alludes to the change in Antonio's face. Antonio falls silent.

considered seat of the emotions

deaden   killing (groans were thought to drain lifeblood from the heart)

i.e. like a stone effigy

thought to be caused by excess yellow bile, producing irritability

i.e. acquire a stiff expression

stagnant

assume an obstinate silence

reputation

deep thought

as if to say   as wise as an oracle

no inferior interrupt me

82-105 Gratiano plays the fool by drawing Antonio's attention to his silence, comparing it to being dead. He then makes an appeal to emotional frankness '(I love thee and 'tis my love that speaks)'. Is there a frisson between Antonio and Bassanio? Is this the trouble between them? Gratiano gets no response, so his fool's story goes on: is Antonio being silent to appear wise? Antonio's lack of response causes Gratiano to lose his way.

He raises the stakes by blurting out 'O my Antonio'. Gratiano gets no reaction from Antonio, and winds up his peroration with 'I'll tell thee more of this another time'. He changes tack and admonishes Antonio the way a parent might their child. He expects to see Antonio after dinner.

What is the difference between Solanio and Salerio's efforts, and Gratiano's? Is Gratiano a knowing fool who plays foolish, or a foolish fool who struggles to be knowing, although ending up foolish—and what are Antonio's and Bassanio's reactions? Are they locked into each other's gaze? or indulgent towards him?

O my Antonio, I do know of these
That therefore only are reputed wise
For saying nothing, when I am very sure
If they should speak, would almost damn those ears
Which, hearing them, would call their brothers fools.°
I'll tell thee more of this another time.
But fish not with this melancholy bate°
For this fool gudgeon,° this opinion.°—
Come, good Lorenzo. —Fare ye well awhile,
I'll end my exhortation after dinner.

LORENZO Well, we will leave you then till dinnertime.
I must be one of these same dumb wise men,
For Gratiano never lets me speak.

GRATIANO Well, keep me company but two years more,
Thou shalt not know the sound of thine own tongue.

ANTONIO Fare you well, I'll grow a talker for this gear.°

GRATIANO Thanks i'faith, for silence° is only commendable
In a neat's tongue dried° and a maid not vendible.°

Exeunt [GRATIANO and LORENZO.]

ANTONIO Yet is that anything now?°

BASSANIO Gratiano speaks an infinite deal of nothing more than any man in all Venice. His reasons are as two grains of wheat hid in two bushels of chaff: you shall seek all day ere you find them, and when you have them they are not worth the search.

ANTONIO Well, tell me now what lady is the same°
To whom you swore a secret pilgrimage
That you today promised to tell me of.

BASSANIO 'Tis not unknown to you, Antonio,
How much I have disabled° mine estate
By something° showing° a more swelling port°
Than my faint means would grant continuance,°
Nor do I now make moan to be abridged
From such a noble rate;° but my chief care
Is to come fairly off° from the great debts

cause hearers to call them fools and risk damnation (cf. Matthew 5:22)

show of gravity

gullible fool reputation (for intelligence)

business, chat

i.e. sexual inactivity

i.e. impotent old man marketable; i.e. marriage-able

But what's the point of that here?

the one

depleted

somewhat sporting ex-travagant lifestyle

allow to continue

about being cut back of lavish spending

clear myself honorably

106-111 Certainly Lorenzo's lines suggest humour and tolerance: when Gratiano bids one to go, one must go, even if, when 'I' bid him go, 'we' did not go. Gratiano jokes back about 'dumbness', to 'not know the sound of thine own tongue', again highlighting Antonio's silence. Is Antonio joining in the jest by suggesting that Gratiano's 'infinite deal of nothing' might drive him to talk (l.111)?

112-119 Line 114 is a short line, then do Antonio and Bassanio use it to watch Lorenzo and Gratiano go? or is something happening between them that won't allow Bassanio to speak?

Bassanio avails himself of Antonio's 'small talk' and lowers the emotional temperature by speaking in prose. These lines give the audience a respite from verse, allowing itself to prepare for the encounter to come. Both speak about Gratiano, thereby keeping the subject matter away from themselves. Antonio brings the play straightway back to verse.

120-135 Antonio's 'well' may mark delay, but it is clear that Bassanio has broached the subject of a woman, that he is leaving Venice, and that he has 'promised ' to tell Antonio all today. Is this the cause of Antonio's 'sadness'? Notice that Antonio has only ever reacted to other characters; here he takes the initiative.

Bassanio raises the subject and then delays conversation. Does this mean he is secretive? or is he embarrassed? or manipulative? raising a subject on one occasion and leaving it to settle into Antonio's mind? What dramatic tension underlies their encounter? Is it sexual?

Might the situation be more complex? Solanio says that Bassanio is Antonio's 'most noble kinsman'. Are they related through blood? Bassanio needs to tell him of his secret pilgrimage, yet Antonio has been difficult to find. Might there be a part of Antonio that wishes to delay meeting Bassanio?

Bassanio's speech immediately embraces verse, but begins formally, avoiding a direct answer to Antonio.Throughout he talks of debts. He intends to clear his, but in the last four lines couples Antonio with money and love—one of the play's major concerns. Antonio can understand from Bassanio's speech, that once cleared of his debts, his love for him will remain constant.

Wherein my time,° something too prodigal,
Hath left me gaged.° To you, Antonio,
I owe the most in money and in love,
And from your love I have a warranty°
To unburden all my plots° and purposes
How to get clear of all the debts I owe.

ANTONIO I pray you, good Bassanio, let me know it;
And if it stand as you yourself still do,
Within the eye of honor,° be assured
My purse, my person, my extremest means
Lie all unlocked to your occasions.°

BASSANIO In my schooldays, when I had lost one shaft,°
I shot his fellow° of the selfsame flight°
The selfsame way, with more advised° watch
To find the other forth,° and by adventuring° both
I oft found both. I urge this childhood proof°
Because what follows is pure innocence.°
I owe you much, and like a wilful° youth,
That which I owe is lost; but if you please
To shoot another arrow that self° way
Which you did shoot the first, I do not doubt
As I will watch the aim, or° to find both
Or bring your latter hazard° back again,
And thankfully rest debtor for the first.

ANTONIO You know me well, and herein spend but° time
To wind about my love° with circumstance;°
And out of° doubt you do me now more wrong
In making question° of my uttermost°
Than if you had made waste of all I have.
Then do but say to me what I should do
That in your knowledge may by me be done,
And I am pressed unto° it. Therefore speak.

BASSANIO In Belmont is a lady richly left,°
And she is fair, and fairer° than that word,
Of wondrous virtues. Sometimes° from her eyes
I did receive fair speechless messages.
Her name is Portia, nothing undervalued
To° Cato's daughter, Brutus' Portia,°

past
liable

authorization
disclose all my plans

your proposal is as honorable as yourself
needs

shot one arrow
its double   same dimensions, range
careful
out   risking
experience, test
ingenuousness, sincerity
headstrong

same

either
final risk

merely waste
to tease out my affection
unnecessary talk
beyond
doubting   fullest concern

ready to do
who has inherited a large fortune
(even) better
once

of no less worth than
famous for intelligence, loyalty and integrity (see Caesar II.i.233-309)

136-153 Urged by Antonio to tell him his plan, Bassanio again delays, by choosing a homily from his school days about bows and arrows. It is as if Bassanio's is a rehearsed speech.

He has now failed to answer Antonio's first question or acknowledge the offer in his second speech: is Bassanio incapable, or does he deliberately avoid coming to the point?

154-161 Antonio loses patience with Bassanio's temporising. As if Bassanio's delay is a sign he doubts him. Doubting his integrity, friendship, and love is worse than if he had bankrupted him. He admonishes Bassanio with the extended hand of friendship.

Notice the difference in register. Antonio's address is direct, courteous, tough, underpinned by love and friendship in contrast to Bassanio's formality. The longer Bassanio takes to come to the point, the more doubt is generated.

162-177 Bassanio comes to the point. Note the enthusiasm, the unbottling, the rhythmic change in Bassanio's language. In Belmont, a fictitious place (in contrast to Venice), is a woman richly left, beautiful and with wondrous virtues. Bassanio has met her, knows her name and she has given him encouragement with her eyes. As if, in fear of betraying too much enthusiasm, he turns to a cooler classical style, compares her to Brutus' Portia who is renowned for intelligence and loyalty. Suitors come from all corners of the world to win her.

The mercantile language and the language of love wind around each other. To Antonio he speaks first of her worth and then of her beauty and virtue. Where does the balance lie between his earlier statement that he wishes to clear his debts, and his love for Portia? Is he telling Antonio that he wishes to love both a man and a woman? The language seems calculated to leave Antonio wondering where the balance between money and love lies. The suggestion is that you need to make a display because many famous 'renowned' suitors come from everywhere, but they also come because she is rich.

With the 'O' here, Bassanio shows the depth of his need to have his request granted, and he moves from the 'you Antonio' to 'my Antonio'. Bassanio is convinced he will be fortunate.

Nor is the wide world ignorant of her worth,
For the four winds blow in from every coast
Renownèd suitors, and her sunny locks
Hang on her temples like a golden fleece,
Which makes her seat° of Belmont Colchis' strand,°
And many Jasons come in quest of her.
O my Antonio, had I but the means
To hold a rival place with one of them,
I have a mind presages me such thrift°
That I should questionless be fortunate.

ANTONIO Thou know'st that all my fortunes are at sea,
Neither have I money nor commodity°
To raise a present sum.° Therefore go forth,
Try what my credit can in Venice do°—
That shall be racked° even to the uttermost
To furnish thee to Belmont to fair Portia.
Go presently° inquire, and so will I,
Where money is, and I no question make°
To have it of my trust° or for my° sake. *Exeunt.*

Scene ii Enter PORTIA with her waiting-woman° NERISSA.

PORTIA By my troth,° Nerissa, my little body is aweary of this great world.

NERISSA You would be, sweet madam, if your miseries were in the same abundance as your good fortunes are; and yet for aught° I see, they are as sick that surfeit° with too much as they that starve with nothing. It is no mean° happiness therefore to be seated in the mean;° superfluity° comes sooner° by white hairs,° but competency° lives longer.

PORTIA Good sentences,° and well pronounced.°

NERISSA They would be better if well followed.

PORTIA If to do were as easy as to know what were good to do, chapels had been° churches, and poor men's cottages princes'

country estate shore on the Black sea where Jason led the Argonauts to win the Golden Fleece

premonitions of such profit, success

merchandise

ready money

will fetch in Venice

stretched

immediately

do not doubt

credit (as a merchant) friendship's

178-186 One can play this scene between Antonio and Bassanio as an older friend happy to oblige the younger. But then the scene lacks tension. Why would an older man lend a great deal of money unless there is a sexual tension between them? Has this love been consummated? or is it an infatuation which exists on a homoerotic level? or if there has been a homosexual relationship does Bassanio now desire to move into a heterosexual one: with any of these Antonio will lose Bassanio, or at best share him with a woman.

Despite Bassanio's awareness that all Antonio's fortune is tied up at sea, he still asks for help. Does Antonio desperately wish to help Bassanio as the way of keeping him?

While being true to his word, and twice telling him to 'go' it is as if Antonio can't bear to be in Bassanio's presence. The urgency of the situation is underlined by both leaving the stage in separate directions. There is no indication that Antonio's sadness is lifting.

Scene ii

friend, confidante

faith

anything gorge themselves

slight

between extremes lavishness (and anxiety)

sooner gains i.e. premature wisdom (about how much is enough) modest sufficiency

maxims spoken (Portia may be mocking)

would be

1-8 Two women enter but we do not know who or where they are. One is called Nerissa, and she calls the other 'sweet Madam': these words, with their appearances, may indicate that Madam is the rich Portia. Notice how Nerissa builds her speech through antithesis. When the other woman replies is she grateful or sarcastic?

What do we learn in these opening lines? First that the women speak in prose giving the audience a change, that the unnamed woman is more powerful than Nerissa. Nerissa tries to moderate her opinion, like a mother with a teenage daughter. Nerissa's speech takes the other woman's 'aweary of this great world' seriously, even if her strategy is to buoy her up: in Jude Kelly's 1994 production for the West Yorkshire Playhouse, Leeds, England, Portia swigs wine and fires an unloaded gun into her own mouth.

9-18 The first woman throws back Nerissa's antithesis: she too can work with words, yet concludes that 'this reasoning' will not get her a husband.

palaces. It is a good divine° that follows his own instructions. I can easier teach twenty what were good to be done than to be one of the twenty to follow mine own teaching. The brain may devise laws° for the blood,° but a hot temper° leaps o'er a cold decree°—such a hare is madness the youth° to skip o'er° the meshes° of good counsel the cripple.° But this reasoning is not in the fashion° to choose me a husband. Oh me the word "choose"! I may neither choose who I would nor refuse who I dislike, so is the will° of a living daughter curbed by the will° of a dead father. Is it not hard, Nerissa, that I cannot choose one nor refuse none?

NERISSA Your father was ever virtuous, and holy men at their death have good inspirations; therefore the lottery that he hath devised in these three chests of gold, silver, and lead, whereof° who chooses his meaning° chooses you, will no doubt never be chosen by any rightly but one who you shall rightly love. But what warmth is there in your affection towards any of these princely suitors that are° already come?

PORTIA I pray thee overname° them, and as thou namest them, I will describe them, and according to my description level° at my affection.

NERISSA First there is the Neapolitan prince.

PORTIA Ay, that's a colt° indeed, for he doth nothing but talk of his horse, and he makes it a great appropriation to his own good parts° that he can shoe him himself. I am much afeard my lady his mother played false° with a smith.

NERISSA Then is there the County° Palatine.

PORTIA He doth nothing but frown, as who should° say, "And° you will not have me, choose." He hears merry tales and smiles not; I fear he will prove the weeping philosopher° when he grows old, being so full of unmannerly° sadness in his youth. I had rather be married to a death's-head with a bone in his mouth° than to either of these. God defend me from these two!

NERISSA How say you by° the French lord, Monsieur le Bon?

PORTIA God made him, and therefore let him pass for a man. In truth I know it is a sin to be a mocker, but he—why, he hath a

clergyman

controls emotions
passionte temperament

reasoned decision

lusty youth easily elude
hunting nets; i.e. restraints
those prudent but impotent

useful to help

wish, sexual desire

testament, wish

among which whoever
intended chest (representing
Portia)

have

run through

guess

inexperienced and foolish
youth

addition to his own talents

illicitly

Count. Portia's description
seems to correspond to the
Elizabethan stereotype of a
Spaniard

as if to if

Heraclitus of Ephesus (c.540-
480 BC), reputed as a
melancholy and misan-
thropic recluse; he was contrasted with the "laughing
philosopher" Democritus

unbecoming

referring to the figure of a
skull and cross-bones

about

19-23 We're beginning to understand a context—the other woman's speech jump-cuts around, has an impatience which suggests youthfulness; she can argue with Nerissa on her own terms and is therefore educated; she's rich, yet cannot choose a husband: although yet unnamed in the dialogue, the audience know Portia is speaking.

Right away, her 'O me' and her 'aweary' indicates that she cannot choose the one or refuse the other. We already know that suitors are coming from all shores to win Portia—now we see the effect this is having on her.

24-29 Nerissa promotes Portia's father's reasoning as a way of reassuring Portia: but note the black humour. At his death he has good 'inspirations' (breathes just as he expires) when setting up a lottery for his daughter's hand. These words set the scene and explain the central device of the three chests.

30-68 What's the dramatic reason for Nerissa asking Portia about her feelings toward the princely suitors? Surely they both know. So that Portia can unburden herself? as a way to vent her feelings and make the situation bearable? This scene is a waiting scene: for the next suitors to arrive or leave. This is also a scene of girls' talk where being impolite releases laughter and pressure.

As the suitors are listed, Portia becomes more and more outrageous in her sexual puns, innuendoes and opinions. While Nerissa's manner and body might make a comment, she stays silent except to prompt Portia to the next suitor.

horse better than the Neapolitan's, a better bad habit of frowning than the Count Palatine, he is every man° in no man. If a throstle° sing, he falls straight a-capering.° He will fence with his own shadow. If I should marry him, I should marry twenty husbands. If° he would despise me, I would forgive him, for if he love me to madness, I shall never requite him.

NERISSA What say you then to Falconbridge, the young baron of England?

PORTIA You know I say nothing to him, for he understands not me nor I him. He hath neither Latin, French, nor Italian, and you will come into the court and swear° that I have a poor pennyworth in the English.° He is a proper man's picture,° but alas who can converse with a dumb show? How oddly he is suited!° I think he bought his doublet° in Italy, his round hose° in France, his bonnet° in Germany, and his behavior everywhere.

NERISSA What think you of the Scottish lord his neighbor?

PORTIA That he hath a neighborly charity in him, for he borrowed a box of the ear of the Englishman and swore he would pay him again when he was able. I think the Frenchman became his surety and sealed under for another.°

NERISSA How like you the young German, the Duke of Saxony's nephew?

PORTIA Very vilely in the morning when he is sober, and most vilely in the afternoon when he is drunk. When he is best he is a little worse than a man, and when he is worst he is little better than a beast. And° the worst fall° that ever fell,° I hope I shall make shift° to go without him.

NERISSA If he should offer to choose, and choose the right casket, you should refuse to perform your father's will, if you should refuse to accept him.

PORTIA Therefore for fear of the worst, I pray thee set a deep glass of Rhenish wine° on the contrary° casket, for if the devil be within and that temptation without, I know he will choose it. I will do anything, Nerissa, ere I will be married to a sponge.

NERISSA You need not fear, lady, the having any of these lords; they have acquainted me with their determinations, which

imitates everybody else while lacking a character of his own

thrush immediately begins 1) trilling 2) dancing about

even if

can testify

precious little knowledge of English appears handsome

dressed. Portia echoes satires of the Elizabethan gentleman's reputation for aping foreign fashions close-fitting upper garment, similar to a Jacket short padded-out breeches

soft round hat

backer for retaliation and pledged himself to give the Englishman an extra box on the ear

if happen were to happen

manage

Rhine wine, admired for its intense ("deep") bouquet wrong

69-82 The tone changes with the Duke of Saxony's nephew, an abusive alcholic who Portia loathes. This catalogue of faults in the suitors gives context to Portia's tension: she is to be won in a lottery, gain a husband, and anyone on this list would be appalling. It's funny, it's over the top, but also deadly serious.

More choices for a production: Nerissa's speech about gold, silver or lead caskets is for the benefit of the audience and not for Portia, so where is the dramatic tension? The speech introduces several points: the choice is not automatic; these are now 'caskets' note 'chests'; and the phrase 'right caskets' intrigues since it indicates that the women know what's in them.

However funny Portia is in extremity, she fears 'the worst'—her death, should Saxony chooses correctly. She too speaks of the chest as a casket. She chafes at her father's will, and is prepared to influence and manipulate the situation to get the outcome she wants.

83-92 Nerissa reassures Portia that these suitors are going home before they choose, which suggests there are additional conditions in the will. Nerissa's speech shows her importance in running Belmont: all the suitors (counts, lords, princes) have to deal with her, someone not of their class. We begin to under-

is indeed to return to their home and to trouble you with no more suit unless you may be won by some other sort° than your father's imposition,° depending on the caskets.

PORTIA If I live to be as old as Sibylla,° I will die as chaste as Diana° unless I be obtained by the manner of my father's will. I am glad this parcel° of wooers are so reasonable, for there is not one among them but I dote on° his very absence, and I pray God grant them a fair departure.

NERISSA Do you not remember, lady, in your father's time, a Venetian, a scholar and a soldier,° that came hither in company of the Marquis of Montferrat?

PORTIA Yes, yes, it was Bassanio—as I think so was he called.°

NERISSA True, madam. He of all the men that ever my foolish eyes looked upon was the best deserving a fair lady.

PORTIA I remember him well, and I remember him worthy of thy praise.

Enter a SERVINGMAN.

How now, what news?

SERVINGMAN The four strangers° seek for you, madam, to take their leave, and there is a forerunner° come from a fifth, the Prince of Morocco, who brings word the prince his master will be here tonight.

PORTIA If I could bid the fifth welcome with so good heart as I can bid the other four farewell, I should be glad of his approach. If he have the condition° of a saint and the complexion of a devil,° I had rather he should shrive me° than wive me. Come, Nerissa. [To SERVINGMAN.] Sirrah,° go before. Whiles we shut the gate upon one wooer, another knocks at the door.

Exeunt.

way

expressed conditions

Deiphobe of Cumae, a prophetess. Apollo promised her years of life equal to the number of grains of sand she could hold in her hand

goddess of chastity

lot

relish

ideal complementary accomplishments in the Renaissance man

Portia plays down her initial enthusiasm

foreigners. Nerissa actually named six suitors; Shakespeare may have added two but forgot to make a correction

herald

character

Devils were portrayed as black, but complexion could also mean "disposition." hear my confession

form of address to social inferiors

stand that she must have been trusted by the father. Seeing Portia's real distress and knowing that any one of these suitors can win her, why does she withold information that could ease some of the suffering? Is she is manipulative, sadistic? or is she teaching Portia that her father's will is working?

The scene takes place in the casket room illustrating the core of Portia's predicament. It is isolation. Suitors come to Belmont by boat. A beautiful heiress sits waiting to be won by the choice of the right casket because of the will of a dead father. While the actors have to respond in a real way, the situation itself feels unreal, a fairy tale or romance. As we witness Portia's frustration we know that Bassanio is preparing to set sail.

93-100 Having calmed and reassured Portia, Nerissa probes further about a Venetian scholar and soldier. Is Portia's resistance solely resistance or informed by her liking of someone else? Portia falls for Nerissa's strategy. She joyously gives herself away by saying 'Yes', realises what she has said, pulls back and feigns coolness. Nerissa is not fooled, but plays it Portia's way. Portia's reaction confirms what Bassanio has told Antonio—that he has encouragement. This speech begins to bind the stories of Venice and Belmont together.

101-111 The entrance of a servingman brings the scene back to the present. If Nerissa's intention at the beginning of the scene had been to ask permission for the suitors to leave, the servingman is there to remind her. Now there is a fifth (by my count seventh) suitor, the Prince of Morocco. This puts Portia under renewed strain and builds tension in the audience. If Bassanio doesn't move fast another suitor may win her.

Scene iii Enter BASSANIO with SHYLOCK the Jew.

SHYLOCK Three thousand ducats,° well.

BASSANIO Ay, sir, for three months.

SHYLOCK For three months, well.

BASSANIO For the which as I told you, Antonio shall be bound.°

SHYLOCK Antonio shall be become bound, well.

BASSANIO May you stead me?° Will you pleasure° me? Shall I know your answer?

SHYLOCK Three thousand ducats for three months, and Antonio bound.

BASSANIO Your answer to that.

SHYLOCK Antonio is a good° man.

BASSANIO Have you heard any imputation to the contrary?

SHYLOCK Ho no, no, no, no; my meaning in saying he is a good man, is to have you understand me that he is sufficient.° Yet his means are in supposition:° he hath an argosy bound to Tripolis, another to the Indies; I understand, moreover, upon the Rialto,° he hath a third at Mexico, a fourth for England, and other ventures he hath squandered° abroad. But ships are but boards, sailors but men; there be land rats and water rats, water thieves and land thieves—I mean pirates°—and then there is the peril of waters, winds, and rocks. The man is notwithstanding sufficient: three thousand ducats. I think I may take his bond.

BASSANIO Be assured you may.

SHYLOCK I will be assured° I may, and that I may be assured, I will bethink me.° May I speak with Antonio?

BASSANIO If it please you to dine with us.

Scene iii

gold coins, usually of high value

under legal obligation

Can you help me? oblige

financially sound, but Bassanio understands "honorable"

a good credit risk, well-to-do

assumed but not certain

the mercantile Exchange of Venice famous for its bridge

1) spread 2) cast recklessly

Shylock puns on "rats" pi-rats

have no doubt; Shylock implies he will also demand legal assurances

carefully consider the matter; or Shylock may already have an idea and suddenly ask "May I speak..."

1-11 Scene three begins in mid-conversation: Bassanio is going over the information a second time for Shylock; he needs convincing. Note the change of 'be' to 'become' (l.5). Does this encourage Bassanio because it implies the definite future, hinting that the part of the deal that interests Shylock is that 'Antonio shall become bound'? Whether a business tactic or pondering, Shylock has to be asked three times for an answer. The third time Bassanio makes a demand, suggesting urgency.

12-23 Shylock's 'Antonio is a good man' implies that he is commercially sound, he is honourable, and also he is below the rank of a gentleman. Shylock answers in financial not emotional terms; plays at uncertainty with Bassanio by pondering, then giving an answer then qualifying with a 'yet'. Shylock seems remarkably well-informed of Antonio's merchant business and corroborates Antonio's 'all my fortunes are at sea' (1.1.178).

Is 'other ventures he hath squand'red abroad' a dig at Antonio's indulgence of Bassanio?

24-26 Bassanio's 'assur'd' is an emotional response but Shylock replies in a financial way, needing a guarantee, and asks to see Antonio. The 1998 Shakespeare's Globe production in London went down another path by making Shylock a stage villain from the outset. Michael Billington wrote "Last Friday afternoon I heard a Jew being hissed at in south London...I began to wonder whether one effect of this new theatre is to morally simplify Shakespeare's plays and turn them into a form of Victorian melodrama" (The Guardian, 1998). Neil Smith adds: "Kentrup turns Shylock into the kind of cackling villain rarely seen outside the confines of pantomime...For the most part he plays to the gallery, justifying himself to the audience and treating us as colluding confidantes" (What's On, 1998).

27-32 Shylock's reply depends on how he reacts to Bassanio's offer 'to dine with us'. Are these lines an aside, or spoken directly to Bassanio? Is this invitation hypocrisy on Bassanio's part? For the first time in the play Shylock foregrounds his Jewishness. His outburst may come from the fact that Antonio despises him, and Bassanio would know this. But if Bassanio does know then why does he go to Shylock? Does Shylock allow himself the outburst

SHYLOCK Yes, to smell pork, to eat of the habitation which° your prophet the Nazarite° conjured the devil into. I will buy with you, sell with you, talk with you, walk with you, and so following, but I will not eat with you, drink with you, nor pray with you. What news on the Rialto? Who is he comes here?

Enter ANTONIO.

BASSANIO This is Signor Antonio.

[ANTONIO and BASSANIO talk apart.]

SHYLOCK How like a fawning publican° he looks.
I hate him for° he is a Christian;
But more for that in low simplicity°
He lends out money gratis,° and brings down
The rate of usance° here with us in Venice.
If I can catch him once upon the hip,°
I will feed fat the ancient grudge I bear him.
He hates our sacred nation, and he rails
Even there where merchants most do congregate
On me, my bargains, and my well-won thrift,°
Which he calls interest. Cursed be my tribe
If I forgive him.

BASSANIO Shylock, do you hear?

SHYLOCK I am debating of my present store,°
And by the near guess of my memory
I cannot instantly raise up the gross°
Of full three thousand ducats. What of that?
Tubal, a wealthy Hebrew of my tribe,
Will furnish me. But soft,° how many months
Do you desire? [To ANTONIO.] Rest you fair, good signor,
Your worship was the last man in our mouths.°

ANTONIO Shylock, albeit I neither lend nor borrow
By taking nor by giving of excess,°
Yet to supply the ripe wants° of my friend,
I'll break a custom. [To BASSANIO.] Is he yet possessed°
How much ye would?°

SHYLOCK Ay, ay, three thousand ducats.

into which

Jesus, who cast out evil spirits into a herd of Swine (Mark 5:1-13)

Shylock seems to mean "two-faced:" publicans were the Roman tax collectors loathed by the Jews, but one described by Luke 18:10-14 prayed humbly for mercy; Antonio conceals his usual scorn with an ingratiating ("fawning") air because he seeks a favor

because

humble foolishness, or contemptible folly

interest-free

interest, usury

at a disadvantage

prosperity

deliberating about my supply of ready money

full amount

wait a moment

i.e. we were just talking about you, sir. Shylock's delayed greeting to Antonio may suggest his underlying dislike

of excess with interest charges

pressing needs

informed

need

because he has the power and Bassanio needs the loan. Is Shylock simply saying: don't mix business with pleasure.

33-44 Shylock, while on the surface wishing to know the news on the Rialto and who comes here, may be gloating that Antonio might be in his power.

As Antonio enters Bassanio introduces him to Shylock, who chooses not to hear but goes into an aside instead, deliberately slighting Antonio and raising intensity by using verse. Since Bassanio introduces Antonio to Shylock, does this confirm that Bassanio doesn't know they know each other?

Shylock's 'fawning publican', explored on its own, is both a comment on Antonio's relationships to Bassanio and how Shylock feels he has to conduct himself in Antonio's presence. In this direct address to the audience, does he confess intended action, or debate about action? Does Shylock hate Antonio for his Christianity or for lending money out gratis, or are the two inextricably linked?

Shylock's language shows he feels himself in combat with Antonio. He conflates the interest of the Jewish nation with himself. Antonio often berates him in the most public of places, although Bassanio doesn't seem to know. Shylock thinks himself a merchant, yet Antonio will not accept him as such, and insists he is something other.

45-53 Bassanio asks 'Shylock, do you hear?'. Has he been waiting patiently or is he interrupting? Does Shylock pretend not to have heard Bassanio and therefore not seen Antonio? or does he see Antonio but deliberately ignore him to his face? Is this Shylock's strategy to see how badly the money is needed?

When Shylock clearly masks his aside (l.46) with a lie, we begin to wonder if he is trustworthy. Whatever the rights or wrongs of his treatment at Antonio's hand, he is going to retaliate. When Shylock suggests that he does not have enough cash it is both a tactic to unsettle Bassanio and lets Antonio know that the 'usurer' himself needs to borrow.

When Shylock at last acknowledges Antonio, he carries on the language of the aside. 'I will feed fat' and the 'last man in our mouths' marries up the aside and his reply, conveying them (if in a hidden way) to Antonio.

54-61 Antonio knows Shylock—they have

ANTONIO And for three months.

SHYLOCK I had forgot—[To BASSANIO.] three months, you told me so
Well then, your bond, and let me see—but hear you,
Methoughts° you said you neither lend nor borrow
Upon advantage.°

ANTONIO I do never use° it.

SHYLOCK When Jacob grazed his uncle Laban's sheep°—
This Jacob from our holy Abram° was
[As his wise mother wrought in his behalf.]
The third possessor;° ay, he was the third—

ANTONIO And what of him, did he take interest?

SHYLOCK No, not take interest, not as you would say
Directly interest. Mark what Jacob did:
When Laban and himself were compromised°
That all the eanlings° which were streaked and pied°
Should fall° as Jacobs hire, the ewes being rank°
In end of autumn turned to the rams;
And when the work of generation was
Between these woolly breeders in the act,
The skillful shepherd peeled° me° certain wands
And, in the doing of the deed of kind,°
He stuck them up before the fulsome° ewes,
Who then conceiving did in eaning° time
Fall° parti-colored lambs, and those were Jacob's.
This was a way to thrive, and he was blessed,
And thrift is blessing if men steal it not.

ANTONIO This was a venture,° sir, that Jacob served for,°
A thing not in his power to bring to pass,
But swayed and fashioned by the hand of heaven.
Was this inserted to make interest good?°
Or is your gold and silver ewes and rams?

SHYLOCK I cannot tell, I make it breed as fast.
But note me, signor—

ANTONIO Mark you this, Bassanio,
The devil can cite Scripture for his purpose.
An evil soul producing holy witness

it seemed to me

by charging interest

1) make a practice of 2) take usury = interest

Shylock's story of Jacob increasing his portion of Laban's flock was based on the belief that offspring will resemble whatever their mother sees at the moment of conception. See Genesis 30:25-43

the original name of Abraham (Genesis 11:26)

i.e. holder of the family rights of inheritance after Abraham and Issac

agreed

new-born lambs spotted, parti-colored (see l.81)

be allotted as Jacob's share in heat

partly stripped the bark off some branches; "me" is a chatty interjection meaning roughly "according to my report"

act of copulation

fertile, lustful

lambing

give birth to

unpredictable undertaking worked for (as a servant of his uncle Laban and of God). Antonio counters Shylock with the spiritual interpretation of Jacob's actions (Genesis 31:1-16)

example introduced in order to justify usury?

clashed over usury or 'excess'. The deliberate ignoring of Antonio may be Shylock's strategy, but is it also a reaction? as was his outward silence when kicked in the Rialto?

Shylock doesn't give Bassanio the chance to reply to Antonio but jumps in. Having got Antonio's attention, Shylock continues thinking out loud, slowing things down and not seeming too eager—line 59 is a short line, there is a silence Shylock must somehow command.

In many productions it is fashionable to play Antonio and his coterie as anti-semitic bully-boys. But Peter Zadek's production for the Berliner Ensemble, Germany took a different tack. John Peter saw it as: "This is a society where anti-semitism has been refined into polite, sinuous understatement. Gert Voss's Shylock is a totally assimilated Jew—smooth, composed and worldly, not remotely semitic looking, and already used to people needing his services. When the Christians taunt him, it is done suavely" (Sunday Times,1995).

62-86 Given his beliefs about usury, is Antonio committing a form of suicide? Note how Shylock uses the euphemism 'advantage' when he means usury or interest. Shylock tells the story of how Jacob engenders a great deal of something out of nothing by putting peeled wands in front of ewes during conception. Is this how Portia too is won? Put caskets in front of suitors' eyes, choose right and you get to keep Portia? Bassanio stays quiet because he needs money; but why does Antonio, unless he's waiting to hear about the bond? Whether Christian or Jew, Shylock's story is one both beliefs share and therefore a point of commonality; yet Antonio argues and questions his motives.

87-95 Shylock chooses not to argue about difference. At the shared line 90, has Shylock finished or does Antonio interrupt him? If Antonio's 'Mark you this Bassanio' is an interruption, then Shylock changes subject back to business, having felt attacked or humiliated. Even if Shylock has finished his speech, it feels like a deliberate denigration or humiliation of Shylock, which he chooses not to confront.

Antonio's outburst is curious because he has made his opposition clear. Yet, by involving Bassanio, he may also be letting Bassanio know the cost he is incurring for being bound. Is Antonio's

Is like a villain with a smiling cheek,
A goodly° apple rotten at the heart.
O what a goodly outside falsehood hath!

SHYLOCK Three thousand ducats, 'tis a good round sum.
Three months from twelve, then let me see the rate—

ANTONIO Well, Shylock, shall we be beholden° to you?

SHYLOCK Signor Antonio, many a time and oft
In the Rialto you have rated° me
About my moneys and my usances.°
Still° have I born it with a patient shrug,
For sufferance° is the badge of all our tribe.
You call me misbeliever, cut-throat dog,
And spit upon my Jewish gaberdine,°
And all for use of that which is mine own.
Well then, it now appears you need my help.
Go to,° then. You come to me and you say
"Shylock, we would have moneys"—you say so,
You that did void your rheum° upon my beard,
And foot° me as you spurn a stranger° cur
Over your threshhold, moneys is your suit.°
What should I say to you? Should I not say
"Hath a dog money? Is it possible
A cur can lend three thousand ducats?" Or
Shall I bend low, and in a bondman's key°
With bated° breath and whispering humbleness,
Say this: "Fair sir, you spat on me on Wednesday last,
You spurned me such a day; another time
You called me dog; and for these courtesies
I'll lend you thus much moneys"?

ANTONIO I am as like to call thee so again,
To spit on thee again, to spurn thee too.
If thou wilt lend this money, lend it not
As to thy friends—for when did friendship take
A breed for barren metal° of his friend? '
But lend it rather to thine enemy,
Who if he break,° thou mayst with better face°
Exact the penalty.

SHYLOCK Why, look you how you storm!

fine-looking

obliged, indebted

abused, reviled

interest on loans

always

endurance, suffering

upper garment like a cape

an expression of unbelieving annoyance like "you must be joking!"

spit

kick   strange dog

request

slavish tone of voice

restrained; i.e. gentle

such unnatural interest on money; i.e. as if inert ("barren") metal could increase itself by breeding

from whom if he default   a more appropriate response

attack on Shylock the way he attacks him in the Rialto? Shylock goes quiet before responding.

96-128 For the first time Shylock brings himself to mention 'Signior Antonio'. He develops publicly what we have already heard him say privately about being rated in public, and we see how much it festers. He interweaves his destiny with that of the Jewish nation. Note that Shylock (publicly) hasn't blown his top before, but now he is incandescent at Antonio's hypocrisy: he wishes to borrow yet is in the habit of spitting on him. Shylock's outburst feels emotional, a lashing out not calculated to go anywhere. He answers by playing the inferior roles—a dog, a bondsman—words that thread themselves through the whole play. From lines 116 to121 does Shylock become the bondsman with bated breath whispering in humbleness?

Bill Alexander's 1988 production for the Royal Shakespeare Company (RSC), England, Victoria Radin writes: "Shylock's remark that Antonio and his gang of young bloods 'void your rheum upon my beard and foot me' is borne out by an Antonio who does indeed spit and kick. In their first scene together he wields his long cane over Shylock's head and tears the abacus out of his hands. A long silence from Shylock follows, after which he asks, 'Hath a dog money?' We see [in Antony Sher's portrayal] a very angry outsider struggling to keep his dignity. When he takes the cane out of Antonio's hands, the Christian group cowers, for they are bullies" (New Statesman, 1988).

In lines 125-129 Antonio maps out the distinction between friendship and enemy. There is an alarming abandonment in Antonio's conduct: hurtful, while still making clear that he wishes to borrow money. In his way, Antonio is as exercised as Shylock.

129-145 Why does Antonio wish to be beholden to Shylock and give him a strategy for revenge? Is Antonio carelessly confident that his ships will come in, or is he a melancholic on the precipice of extremity? how would other merchants judge Antonio's borrowing money from someone he regularly kicks and spits in the Rialto? Is it a bad and desperate joke on Antonio's part?

Shylock's rejoinder 'Why' softens the situation; it almost has a paternal quality to it. Shylock implies he said what he has said to clear the air, to

I would be friends with you and have your love,
Forget the shames that you have stained me with,
Supply your present wants, and take no doit°
Of usance for my monies, and you'll not hear me.
This is kind° I offer.

BASSANIO This were° kindness.

SHYLOCK This kindness will I show.
Go with me to a notary, seal me there
Your single° bond, and, in a merry sport°
If you repay me not on such a day
In such a place, such sum or sums as are
Expressed in the condition,° let the forfeit
Be nominated° for an equal pound
Of your fair flesh, to be cut off and taken
In what part of your body pleaseth me.

ANTONIO Content, in faith. I'll seal to such a bond
And say there is much kindness° in the Jew.

BASSANIO You shall not seal to such a bond for me.
I'll rather dwell° in my necessity.

ANTONIO Why fear not, man, I will not forfeit it.
Within these two months—that's a month before
This bond expires—I do expect return
Of thrice three times the value of this bond.

SHYLOCK O father Abram, what these Christians are,
Whose own hard dealings teaches them suspect
The thoughts of others. [To BASSANIO.] Pray you tell me this:
If he should break his day,° what should I gain
By the exaction of the forfeiture?
A pound of man's flesh taken from a man
Is not so estimable,° profitable neither,
As flesh of muttons, beefs or goats. I say
To buy his favor I extend this friendship.
If he will take it, so; if not, adieu.
And for my love° I pray you wrong me not.°

ANTONIO Yes, Shylock, I will seal unto this bond.

SHYLOCK Then meet me forthwith at the notary's.

small Dutch coin of trifling value

1) kindness 2) a natural willingness (as opposed to the "unnatural" practice of usury—l.126)

would be

single without conditions (e.g. for security) attached; Shylock then immediately adds a condition, apparently on a lark   jest

terms (of the bond)

named as an exact (or just)

natural friendliness

remain content to lack means (for venturing to Belmont)

fail to pay on the due date

valuable

for the sake of my kindness don't 1) treat me unjustly 2) attribute evil motives to me

have Antonio's love, to lend him money without interest, and then accuses Antonio of not 'hearing' him. When Antonio says nothing, Bassanio, with his need for the money, steps in so Shylock's offer does not go unreplied. Note Bassanio's picking up of Shylock's word 'kind'.

There is a dramatic shift in tone between Shylock's last speech and his joking around the 'single bond' as he tries to win Antonio over. In Irving's production, Shylock tapped Antonio confidingly on the chest at these words, Antonio recoiling from his touch. Olivier preserved Irving's gesture, but used it five lines later, at 'your fair flesh'. In David Thacker's production for the RSC, Shylock "becomes an assimilated banker with a laptop on one side of his desk and a Bible on the other and when he proposes the bond it is in jokily ironic, stereotype tones" (The Guardian, 1994). While Shylock will become deadly serious about the bond, there are events between now and the trial that sour him further.

146-173 When Bassanio forbids Antonio to take the bond, does Antonio respond by accepting Shylock's 'single bond' within the spirit of a jest? Shylock continues in a spirit of jocularity because he cannot afford to let Bassanio destroy the bargain.

He works hard to convince Bassanio, yet does Bassanio's failure to answer mean that he's not convinced? Antonio is convinced and from line 163 onwards he speeds the scene along: instructions are given. Shylock is in such a hurry that he leaves on the half line. Note Antonio's play on gentle/gentile Jew. He says it first in Shylock's presence, and then clinches the pun with 'kind' after he has gone. Perhaps Antonio really has changed his mind, or is the repetition ironic? Though not convinced, Bassanio is still not worried enough to scupper the deal.

Give him direction for this merry bond
And I will go and purse the ducats straight,°
See to my house, left in the fearful° guard
Of an unthrifty knave,° and presently°
I'll be with you. Exit.

ANTONIO Hie thee,° gentle° Jew.
The Hebrew will turn Christian, he grows kind.°

BASSANIO I like not fair terms and a villain's mind.

ANTONIO Come on. In this there can be no dismay.°
My ships come home a month before the day. Exeunt.

straight away

untrustworthy

servant instantly

hasten with a pun on "gentile" (as elsewhere throughout the play)

like 1.134: friendly and natural

cause for dismay

ACT II

Scene i [Flourish of cornets.] Enter [the Prince of] MOROCCO, a tawny Moor all in white, and three or four followers accordingly, with PORTIA, NERISSA, and their train.

MOROCCO Mislike me not for my complexion,
The shadowed livery of the burnished sun,°
To whom I am a neighbor and near bred.°
Bring me the fairest° creature northward born,
Where Phoebus'° fire scarce thaws the icicles,
And let us make incision for your love
To prove whose blood is reddest,° his or mine.
I tell thee, lady, this aspect° of mine
Hath feared° the valiant. By my love I swear,
The best-regarded virgins of our clime°
Have loved it too. I would not change this hue
Except to steal your thoughts, my gentle queen.

PORTIA In terms of° choice I am not solely led
By nice direction° of a maiden's eyes.
Besides, the lottery of my destiny°
Bars me the right of voluntary choosing.
But if my father had not scanted° me,
And hedged me by his wit to° yield myself
His wife who wins me by that means I told you,
Yourself, renowned prince, then stood as fair
As any comer I have looked on yet
For my affection.

MOROCCO Even for that I thank you.
Therefore I pray you lead me to the caskets
To try my fortune. By this scimitar°
That slew the Sophy° and a Persian prince

ACT II. Scene i

dark uniform worn by servants of the shining sun; i.e. my dark skin

related

most light-skinned

the sun's

most courageous (red blood= sign of courage)

face

terrified

climate

regards to

fastidious or choosy guidance

i.e. the casket riddle

restricted

either 1) confined, or 2) protected me through his wise intentions

Oriental curved sword

Shah of Persia (Iran)

1-12 Morocco's first line is provocative: is it a response to Portia's reaction to his colour? We are in the casket room once more, although these are yet to be seen. Morocco reassures her, calling himself a 'neighbour' to Phoebus, the sun. The chilling phrase, 'incision for piercing your love' suggests cutting—is Morocco's penis the knife? His boasting continues that with 'this aspect of mine', a reference to both his colour and his penis: he has deflowered the best young girls in Morocco and would not change his colour unless it made a difference to winning her.

13-22 In 1.2 Portia raged against her father's will, here she shields herself with it from Morocco, while implying that he could have hoped had it not been there. It was Orson Welles who thought that Bassanio might play all three suitors in order to be certain of his bounty.

Portia and Nerissa use the first twenty lines to try to understand Morocco, and influence the outcome of his choosing a casket: Portia may look at Morocco because of his complexion, but may also be looking at his self-absorption. From 1.2 we know that Portia/Nerissa are prepared to influence the outcome for one suitor. Is there a casket which will entice Morocco more than another? Morocco has been told the rules of the lottery, onerous enough for the five previous suitors to leave without choosing, which seem not to deter him. Does the chase, conquering another virgin much harder to attain, pre-occupy him?

Lines 20-21 are doublespeak, Portia flatters Morocco, while we know her affections are for Bassanio.

23-42 Portia's flattery is reassuring and encourages his decisiveness to choose. He might pull out his scimitar to show his courage. Note his superlatives, outstare, outbrave, most resolute, most daring, to win Portia. Does he mention the 'Sophy', 'a Persian prince', and 'Sultan Suleiman', all Muslims or

That won three feilds of° Sultan Suleiman,°
I would o'erstare° the sternest eyes that look,
Outbrave the heart most daring on the earth,
Pluck the young sucking cubs from the she-bear,
Yea, mock the lion when 'a° roars for prey,
To win thee, lady. But alas the while,
If Hercules and Lichas° play at dice
Which° is the better man, the greater throw
May turn by fortune° from the weaker hand;
So is Alcides° beaten by his rage,°
And so may I, blind fortune leading me,
Miss that which one unworthier may attain
And die with grieving.

PORTIA You must take your chance
And either not attempt to choose at all
Or swear before you choose, if you choose wrong,
Never to speak to lady afterward
In way of marriage. Therefore be advised.°

MOROCCO Nor will not.° Come bring me unto my chance.

PORTIA First forward to the temple.° After dinner
Your hazard° shall be made.

MOROCCO Good fortune then,
To make me blest or cursed'st among men.
[Flourish of cornets.] Exeunt.

Scene ii Enter [LAUNCELOT GOBBO] the clown,° alone.

LAUNCELOT Certainly my conscience will serve me° to run from this Jew my master. The fiend° is at mine elbow and tempts me, saying to me "Gobbo, Launcelot Gobbo, good Launcelot," or "good Gobbo," or "good Launcelot Gobbo, use your legs, take the start, run away." My conscience says "No, take heed honest Launcelot, take heed honest Gobbo"—or as aforesaid "honest Lancelot Gobbo—do not run, scorn running with thy heels."°

battles over   Suleiman the Magnificent of Turkey, 1520-66
stare down

he

Hercules' page

to determine which

chance

Hercules   ruined by his own wild folly (in gambling at dice)

'infidels', to make himself more desired in Portia's Christian eyes?

Morocco, compares his offer of bravery with the lottery of the caskets—a throw of the dice will not necessarily let the deserving be the winner. Morocco's speech echoes Portia's concerns from 1.2, this time from the wooer's point of view. Yet, in his speech he makes no connection between Portia and the casket. She, in turn, focuses on the conditions of the will. The audience learns that if a suitor chooses, and chooses wrong, he will never marry anyone. Her father's will tries to ensure she is loved, and that nobody chooses without real risk to himself.

When Portia cautions 'be advis'd', Morocco shows he is impetuous or has thought about it beforehand. He agrees to the condition and is impatient to choose.

consider carefully

Nor will I ever (woo another woman if I fail)

i.e. to swear the oaths
venture, chance

43-46 Portia delays, asks Morocco to go to the temple to swear to observe the rules: is she using this extra time to know Morocco better, to direct him to a particular casket?

Scene ii

i.e. the acting company's designated comedian; perhaps also "rustic bumpkin"

1) encourage me 2) be at my disposal

Launcelot imagines his bad and good consciences pleading alternately to win him over

1) with your feet 2) utterly

1-14 2.2 begins mid-scene as Launcelot runs away from Shylock's service. John Russell Brown in the Arden edition suggests that Launcelot is acting out a medieval morality play within which he is the central figure; and in which he can engage the audience directly.

Launcelot's monologue begins with 'certainly' suggesting sure conviction, but we quickly find out he is anything but certain. Line 1 is an example of Shakespeare's internal stage directions requiring the actor 'to run', an instruction reiterated throughout the scene. The devil is at his elbow, a full grown imaginary character. Does repeating Launcelot Gobbo's name suggest this is not the first time the fiend has been at his elbow? Launcelot may play the fiend by jumping either to the left or right of the spot he is standing on; or he can stay on the spot and play

Well, the most courageous fiend bids me pack,° "Via!"° says the fiend, "away!" says the fiend, "for the heavens,° rouse up a brave mind" says the fiend, "and run." Well, my conscience hanging about the neck of my heart says very wisely to me, "My honest friend Launcelot, being an honest man's son," or rather an honest woman's son—for indeed my father did something smack, something grow to, he had a kind of taste°—well, my conscience says "Launcelot, budge not." "Budge" says the fiend. "Budge not" says my conscience. "Conscience" say I, "you counsel well." "Fiend" say I, "you counsel well." To be ruled by my conscience, I should stay with the Jew my master who—God bless the mark°—is a kind of devil; and to run away from the Jew, I should be ruled by the fiend who—saving your reverence—is the devil himself. Certainly the Jew is the very devil incarnation;° and in° my conscience, my conscience is but a kind of hard conscience to offer to counsel me to stay with the Jew. The fiend gives the more friendly counsel. I will run, fiend, my heels are at your commandment, I will run.

Enter old Gobbo with a basket.

be gone go on!

by heavens (an ironic oath for a fiend)

each phrase means "had a taste for lust"

like "saving your reverence" (l.26) an apology for a potentially offensive remark, though here Launcelot is probably not serious: "If you'll pardon my French"

blunder for "incarnate" by

the reaction to hearing the fiend speak. Or is the fiend leading Gobbo away from his spot, to get him away from his 'conscience'?

Gobbo plays 'Conscience' in lines 5 to 7, either at the other side of the spot to where he has been standing, or by playing the reaction to hearing 'Conscience'. The fiend initiates language, Conscience hears it and parries it. Conscience feels like a restraining voice because it doesn't initiate. If the fiend has physically walked Gobbo away, does Conscience bring him back? Gobbo's first line says conscience tells him to run, yet here Conscience says 'do not run'. Perhaps Gobbo was trying to convince his Conscience, whereas here it is speaking to him. The rhythm in lines 8-10 shifts from Conscience's reassurance to the fiend's interruptions—urging, cajoling, ordering Gobbo to run.

In line 9 the fiend speaks in 'heavenly' language: is he having a good laugh? Appropriating Conscience's language to convince Launcelot/ himself? Playing the image of a heavy conscience can inform the actor's action with weight. Conscience continues with 'honest' language, as if not panicked by the fiend.

Launcelot delays conscience's admonition by confessing guilt and making a joke. 'Something grow to' means an erection, 'a kind of taste', indulgence. But why does Launcelot get side-tracked about the sexual prolixities of one parent? Is it that he has not been born 'honest', in wedlock?

15-25 After this three line delay, Conscience, for the first time, takes the initiative, being quite as forceful as the fiend, and tells Launcelot to 'budge not'. There is now a tug of war: budge not—budge—budge not. In line 16 the tug-of war continues, but the point of view changes: Launcelot is being pulled. He may wish to run away, but he is in thrall to whoever counsels him last.

Given the 'Jew' his master has the 'mark' of Cain on him (l 19), how does Launcelot address 'God bless the mark' to his Conscience? and 'saving your reverence' to the fiend? While 'in my conscience' suggests that Launcelot is listening, might he also be saying how difficult it is to endure its expectations? Launcelot states out loud to Conscience that the fiend gives more friendly counsel, as a way to concluding that he will 'run', and obey the devil.

GOBBO Master young man, you, I pray you, which is the way to master Jew's?

LAUNCELOT [Aside.] O heavens, this is my true-begotten father, who being more than sand-blind,° high-gravel-blind,° knows me not. I will try confusions° with him.

GOBBO Master young gentleman, I pray you, which is the way to master Jew's?

LAUNCELOT Turn up on your right hand at the next turning, but at the next turning of all on your left; marry,° at the very next turning, turn of° no hand but turn down indirectly to the Jew's house.

GOBBO Be God's sonties,° 'twill be a hard way to hit. Can you tell me whether one Launcelot that dwells with him, dwell with him or no?

LAUNCELOT Talk you of young Master° Launcelot? [Aside.] Mark me now, now will I raise the waters.°—Talk you of young Master Launcelot?

GOBBO No "master" sir, but a poor man's son. His father, though I say't, is an honest exceeding poor man and, God be thanked, well to live.

LAUNCELOT Well, let his father be what a will, we talk of young Master Launcelot.

GOBBO Your worship's friend, and Launcelot, sir.°

LAUNCELOT But I pray you, ergo° old man, ergo I beseech you, talk you of young Master Launcelot?

GOBBO Of Launcelot, an't° please you mastership.

LAUNCELOT Ergo Master Launcelot. Talk not of Master Launcelot, father,° for the young gentleman, according to Fates and Destinies and such odd sayings, the Sisters Three° and such branches of learning, is indeed deceased, or as you would say in plain terms, gone to heaven.

GOBBO Marry, God forbid! The boy was the very staff of my age, my very prop.

LAUNCELOT [Aside.] Do I look like a cudgel° or a hovel-post,° a staff

half-blind Launcelot's comic extension of "sand-blind;" high = absolutely

blunder for "try conclusions" = make experiments (i.e. invent riddles)

By (the Virgin) Mary; a common Elizabeth oath which had lost its original significance and meant "indeed"

this may be an error in the original text for "turn off"

By God's little saints

as a servant Launcelot cannot claim the title "master," which was reserved for gentlemen

draw tears; i.e. stir up anxiety

Gobbo politely insists upon "Launcelot" without title

therefore; Launcelot affects academic precision

if it

a courteous form of address to an older man; Launcelot has not yet revealed his true identity

in classical mythology the sisters who controlled human destiny; identical with "Fates and Destinies"

short thick baton used as a weapon post for holding up a shelter

26-36 Old Gobbo comes on stage at the tail end of Launcelot's speech. Do lines 28-30 indicate that Launcelot has a cruel streak? or is it bitterness informed by his father putting him into the service of a Jew? Does he continue to act in a play? or is his response some degree of each? 'O heavens!' is both an exclamation of surprise and unexpectedness. Since Launcelot reveals Gobbo is his father in the very moment of running away, we see him disobey his father's will. Perhaps through embarrassment, or to buy the time to evolve a new strategy, he jokes around with him.

37-60 By Gobbo asking for Launcelot, we understand he is looking for the character who is onstage, and that he cannot see. He treats Launcelot with deference, as if he were a gentleman. Notice the sense of difference between Launcelot's earlier description and Gobbo's description of himself as 'honest'. Gobbo's confusion results in silence; he doesn't recognize his son as 'Master' and wonders whether they are speaking of the same person.

Launcelot undercuts Gobbo by bringing him back, but on his terms, to young Master Launcelot. A tussle of wills ensues between father and son: 'young Master Launcelot', 'Launcelot', and 'master Launcelot'.

Launcelot ups the stakes by bringing in latin with the word 'ergo', but Gobbo insists his son is plain Launcelot. Launcelot sets up Gobbo, by twice saying 'we talk' and then knocking it down with 'talk not'. 'Father' is a common form of address to an old man, but here there is a double tension.

In this contest of wills a production needs to solve how best to 'raise the waters' that is, make Gobbo cry. Does the tone change somewhere around lines 49 - 50, to something more 'mock' serious? There is great cruelty in reporting one's death to your father. Does Gobbo break down with 'Marry God forbid!'? In his lament, does he carry the basket? If so, does this make it unintentionally funny? Does the exaggeration of the basket's movement, though humorous, make the grief more complex? Launcelot, seeing the depths of his father's grief, changes tack.

or a prop?—Do you know me father?

GOBBO Alack the day, I know you not young gentleman, but I pray you tell me, is my boy—God rest his soul—alive or dead?

LAUNCELOT Do you not know me, father?

GOBBO Alack sir, I am sand-blind. I know you not.

LAUNCELOT Nay, indeed if you had your eyes you might fail of the knowing me. It is a wise father that knows his own child. Well, old man, I will tell you news of your son. [Kneels.] Give me your blessing. Truth will come to light; murder cannot be hid long—a man's son may—but in the end truth will out.

COBBO Pray you sir, stand up. I am sure you are not Launcelot my boy.

LAUNCELOT Pray you let's have no more fooling about it, but give me your blessing. I am Launcelot your boy that was, your son that is, your child that shall be.°

GOBBO I cannot think you are my son.

LAUNCELOT I know not what I shall think of that, but I am Launcelot the Jew's man, and I am sure Margery your wife is my mother.

GOBBO Her name is Margery indeed. I'll be sworn if thou be Launcelot, thou art mine own flesh and blood. [Feels LAUNCELOT'S head.] Lord—worshipped might he be—what a beard° hast thou got! Thou hast got more hair on thy chin than Dobbin my fill-horse° has on his tail.

LAUNCELOT [Rises.] It should seem then that Dobbin's tail grows backward. I am sure he had more hair of his tail than I have of my face when I last saw him.

GOBBO Lord, how art thou changed! How dost thou and thy master agree? I have brought him a present. How 'gree you now?

LAUNCELOT Well, well;° but for mine own part, as I have set up my rest° to run away, so I will not rest till I have run some ground. My master's a very° Jew. Give him a present? Give him a halter!° I am famished in his service. You may tell° every finger I have with my ribs.° Father, I am glad you are

61-70 Gobbo, grief-stricken, does not connect Launcelot's question with himself, so the humour continues. But Launcelot arguably says line 63 to get Gobbo to understand he is calling him 'father', not just 'old man'.

72-78 Launcelot kneels for a blessing to convince Gobbo he is his son. He tries Biblical references, which lets go of the game and fills in Gobbo's silence. Gobbo tops his unresponsiveness by courteously rejecting Launcelot as his son. Just as there has been an inversion of proverbs 'it is a wise father who knows his own child', there is now an inversion of roles. Launcelot mirrors and directly counters Gobbo's speech. Should 'about it' be spoken in a soft voice to indicate he wishes for no more fooling?

Is the next a testy exchange? Launcelot no longer describes himself as Gobbo's son but as the 'Jew's man, and I am sure Margery/ Your wife is my mother.' Note the 'I am sure' is a riposte to Gobbo's 'I am sure' (l.70). Launcelot remains kneeling.

probably echos the pattern of the Gloria Patris: "As it was in the beginning, is now, and ever shall be;" "child that shall be"= the second childhood of old age

79-86 Gobbo finally touches Launcelot in blessing (lines 80-83), but stage tradition has him touching the back of Launcelot's head which he mistakes for a beard. Gobbo may be blind but he is none too adept with touch either. This is no Jacob tricking Laban, this is Laban tricking himself. Launcelot's beard has more hair than the tail of Dobbin, a fill-horse.

Launcelot again embraces humour as he rises. Is it one of relief, sarcasm, dry affection or all these? Line 85 feels an affectionate dig, evoking his father's blindness even in the days when he could see.

Gobbo mistakes the hair at the back of Launcelot's head for a beard

cart-horse

87-96 There is a rhythmic shift in Gobbo's speech. He is eager, peppering Launcelot with questions, wanting to know everything that has happened and all at once, with the renewed intensity with which one greets a long-parted loved one. The questions show joyous relief that Gobbo has found his son. The lines quickly travel from Launcelot, to Launcelot and his master. Is Gobbo being crafty? Is there, behind his questions, a niggling doubt why he meets Launcelot alone on the street?

Launcelot may mimic Shylock's deliberative expression (see I.iii.1-6)

determined once and for all; "rest" = final wager in Primero, a card game

real

hangman's noose

count

Launcelot comically reverses the usual saying "counting

Launcelot in searching how to begin, reassures with 'Well, well' while buying time to answer. He has made a decision without consulting anyone—breaking his bond of servitude, and his father's will.

Launcelot's mind changes rapidly showing

come. Give me° your present to one Master Bassanio, who indeed gives rare new liveries.° If I serve not him, I will run as far as God has any ground.

Enter BASSANIO with [LEONARDO and] a follower° or two.

O rare fortune, here comes the man! To him, father, for I am a Jew if I serve the Jew any longer.

BASSANIO You may do so, but let it be so hasted° that supper be ready at the farthest° by five of the clock. See these letters delivered, put the liveries to making, and desire Gratiano to come anon° to my lodging. [Exit one of his men.]

LAUNCELOT To him, father.

GOBBO God bless your worship.

BASSANIO Gramercy,° wouldst thou aught° with me?

GOBBO Here's my son sir, a poor boy.

LAUNCELOT Not a poor boy, sir, but the rich Jew's man that would, sir, as my father shall specify.

GOBBO He hath a great infection,° sir, as one would say to serve.

LAUNCELOT Indeed the short and the long is, I serve the Jew, and have a desire as my father shall specify.

GOBBO His master and he—saving your worship's reverence—are scarce cater-cousins.°

LAUNCELOT To be brief, the very truth is, that the Jew having done me wrong, doth cause me, as my father, being I hope an old man, shall frutify° unto you—

GOBBO I have here a dish of doves that I would bestow upon your worship, and my suit is—

LAUNCELOT In very brief, the suit is impertinent° to myself, as your worship shall know by this honest old man, and though I say it, though old man, yet poor man my father.

BASSANIO One speak for both. What would you?

LAUNCELOT Serve you, sir.

one's ribs with one's fingers;" he may spread the fingers of one hand as "ribs" and take hold of Gobbo's hand to count them

on my behalf

splendid new uniforms for his servants

servant and/or acquaintance

hastened

latest

straightaway

many thanks anything

Gobbo's blunder for "affection" = inclination

hardly close friends

Launcelot confuses this with "fructify" though he means "notify;" i.e. inform

blunder for "pertinent"

confusions: he hasn't marshalled a coherent argument. He claims Shylock is starving him, and seizes his father's hand and brings it into contact with his fingers, which are extended rib-like over 'his chest'. The ruse works because his father can neither see nor distinguish the front of his head.

Just as his father once gave Launcelot to Shylock, he now wants Gobbo to give him to Bassanio.

97-103 Bassanio enters as Launcelot finishes. Does 'to him father' become another Launcelot joke? His father neither sees nor hears, so in which direction is he to go?

Bassanio gives instructions, confident and busy; we haven't seen him like this before. Does Bassanio pass by the Gobbos, causing mounting alarm in Launcelot?

104-121 For whatever reasons—confusion, not knowing his bearings, trying to find the moment to interrupt, deliberate indecision, courtesy, class—Gobbo does not interrupt, needing a further exhortation from Launcelot.

In staging the scene the primary conversation is between Old Gobbo and Bassanio, Launcelot is the outsider breaking into their 'circle'.

The juxtaposition between the direct language of the father and the fawning elaborateness of the son continues the comedy. Gobbo embellishes to ridiculous effect. Is he in control of his words? or making a joke at the expense of Launcelot's language? Launcelot loses control of his speaking style, while Old Gobbo asserts an inappropriate intimacy with Bassanio when he confides details of his son's position with Shylock.

When Launcelot interrupts Gobbo, note the joke in his three speeches: he begins 'Indeed the short and the long is' the rest is relatively short; the next begins with 'To be brief' but the speech gets longer, and the third starts 'In very brief' which is the longest yet. The pay off is line 123 when Launcelot, against expectation, answers in just three words. His misconstrued words include 'fruitify' instead of 'fructify': is it here that Gobbo offers Bassanio the present of his basket?

Launcelot gets progressively more flustered and has to work ever harder to keep the conversation going. Gobbo pitches his suit coming better from an 'honest old man', yet goes off message. Bassanio says nothing.

GOBBO That is the very defect° of the matter, sir.

BASSANIO I know thee well, thou hast obtained thy suit.
Shylock thy master spoke with me this day
And hath preferred° thee, if it be preferment
To leave a rich Jew's service to become
The follower of so poor a gentleman.

LAUNCELOT The old proverb° is very well parted° between my master Shylock and you, sir: you have the grace of God, sir, and he hath enough.

BASSANIO Thou speakst it well. Go, father, with thy son.
[To LAUNCELOT.] Take leave of thy old master, and inquire°
My lodging out. [To a servant.] Give him a livery
More guarded° than his fellows'; see it done.

LAUNCELOT Father, in. I cannot get a service, no, I have ne'er a tongue in my head.° [Looks at his palm.] Well, if any man in Italy have a fairer table° which doth offer to swear upon a book, I shall have good fortune. Go to,° here's a simple line of life, here's a small trifle of wives. Alas, fifteen wives is nothing, eleven widows and nine maids is a simple coming-in° for one man. And then to scape° drowning thrice, and to be in peril of my life with the edge of a feather bed°—here are simple scapes.° Well, if fortune be a woman° she's a good wench for this gear.° Father, come, I'll take my leave of the Jew in the twinkling. Exit [LAUNCELOT the] clown [and old GOBBO.]

BASSANIO I pray thee good Leonardo, think on this:
These things being bought and orderly bestowed,°
Return in haste, for I do feast tonight
My best-esteemed acquaintance; hie thee, go.

LEONARDO My best endeavors shall be done herein.

[Makes to leave.]

Enter GRATIANO.

GRATIANO [To LEONARDO.] Where's you master?

LEONARDO Yonder, sir, he walks.

[Exit LEONARDO.]

for "effect" = consequence

recommended for advancement

"He who has the grace of God has enough" shared; i.e. applicable

seek

trimmed with ornamental braid (a jester's coat was also guarded; Bassanio probably employs Launcelot as a fool)

"See if I can't talk my way into success"

palm of the hand; Launcelot begins to read his palm to predict his fortune in marriage

an expression of impatience

modest income (ironic; there may also be a sexual pun)

escape(s)

danger of tumbling out of bed because of my energetic sexual activity (?)

Fortuna was a goddess

i.e. these predictions

neatly stowed on board ship

122-136 Launcelot's speech having come shuddering to a halt, Bassanio effortlessly takes over. Launcelot answering to the point: 'serve you sir'. Gobbo blows it apart with another malapropism, 'defect' instead of 'effect'. The joy here is that Bassanio, having asked 'One speak for both', is undercut by each speaking alone.

As it happens, Shylock has already spoken to Bassanio about taking Launcelot into his service. Does his silence therefore indicate he treats the two for comic entertainment? is he showing courtesy by not interrupting them? or is he making sure that Launcelot wishes to serve him?

The scene helps build a fuller picture of Bassanio: he trusts and accepts Shylock's recommendation; he makes decisions quickly if not with deep reflection since he has only met Shylock, and just met Launcelot—but he needs a retinue to go woo Portia with.

Bassanio speaks about Launcelot's promotion in terms of his livery having more braid than his fellows. Therefore he has permission to play the fool.

137-147 Do Launcelot and Old Gobbo go upstage toward Shylock's house while Bassanio and followers stay onstage? or do they withdraw, leaving the stage clear for the father and son? Launcelot is cock-a-hoop. Does he point Old Gobbo toward Shylock's door while his language bursts with elation? He interrupts himself, self-importantly attributes his good luck entirely to himself, mocks his father, and the would-be fool gloats at his skill with the unselfconsciously ironic 'I cannot get a service, no! I have ne'er a tongue in my head.'

Lines 139-142 direct us to physical actions. 'Table' means the palm of the hand, and so he examines it as if doing palmistry. 'Here's a simple line of life': drowning in women, escape from drowning in water, drowning in a feather-bed. Even when Launcelot ascribes his lines to the Goddess Fortune, he is familiar with her as a 'good wench for this gear'. His self-absorption ends with 'Father come' suggesting Gobbo is about to walk into something, is walking aimlessly, or hasn't moved.

148-157 Bassanio and Leonardo are now alone onstage, or once they re-enter. Note the shift from Bassanio's prose instructions to his followers (before Gobbo's interruption) into verse.

GRATIANO Signor Bassanio.

BASSANIO Gratiano.

GRATIANO I have a suit to you.

BASSANIO You have obtained it.

GRATIANO You must not deny me, I must go with you to Belmont.

BASSANIO Why then you must. But hear thee, Gratiano,
Thou° art too wild, too rude° and bold of voice,
Parts° that become thee happily enough
And in such eyes as ours appear not faults;
But where thou art not known, why, there they show
Something too liberal.° Pray thee, take pain
To allay° with some cold drops of modesty°
Thy skipping° spirit, lest through thy wild behavior
I be misconstered° in the place I go to,
And lose my hopes.

GRATIANO Signor Bassanio, hear me:
If I do not put on a sober habit,°
Talk with respect and swear but now and then,
Wear prayer-books in my pocket, look demurely,
Nay more, while grace is saying hood° mine eyes
Thus with my hat, and sigh and say "amen,"
Use all the observance of civility
Like one well studied in a sad ostent°
To please his grandam,° never trust me more.

BASSANIO Well, we shall see your bearing.

GRATIANO Nay, but I bar tonight. You shall not gauge° me by what we do tonight.

BASSANIO No, that were pity.
I would entreat you rather to put on
Your boldest suit of mirth, for we have friends
That purpose merriment. But fare you well,
I have some business.

GRATIANO And I must to Lorenzo and the rest,
But we will visit you at suppertime. Exeunt.

Gratiano, as asked earlier, doesn't wait to meet Bassanio in his lodging (lines 101-102) but searches him out in the street. He enters in the direction of Leonardo's exit, bumps into him, his prose line being completed with Leonardo's verse. Meanwhile Bassanio exits, and Gratiano runs after him. Again, Gratiano begins with a prose line, which Bassanio completes as verse, granting his request to go to Belmont. Gratiano is so desperate to go, and so out of breath, he does not hear Bassanio and insists on repeating his request as they meet up.

Bassanio switches to second person pronouns indicating familiarity uncouth, coarse (not "impolite")

qualities

unrestrained

temper moderation, decorum

frolicsome, carefree

misconstrued

158-167 As Bassanio says what he thinks of Gratiano, the audience clearly hears its opposite: that Gratiano is not diplomatic, tactful, soft-spoken. Bassanio likes Gratiano but is worried he may put his wooing Portia at risk.

1) behavior 2) attire

cover (hats were worn indoors and during dinner)

practised in appearing sober and earnest

grandmother

judge

168-184 Gratiano's verse becomes ostentatious. He takes up the reference to 'parts', assuring Bassanio that he will become modest. Is Gratiano uncomfortable in the clothes he's being asked to wear although he needs to do so? Or does Gratiano deliberately play with Bassanio by treading the fine line between promising to behave while keeping the threat of 'wild behaviour' alive? or is Gratiano straightforward (while he promises to be modest, he may not know how to do so), leaving Bassanio worried about his potential for misbehaviour? Bassanio gives a rather wan 'yes'. Note that the scene begins with Launcelot casting himself as the chief actor in a medieval play, and ends with Gratiano adopting an extended tableau pose.

Scene iii Enter Jessica and [Launcelot Gobbo] the clown.

Jessica I am sorry thou wilt leave my father so.
Our house is hell, and thou a merry devil
Didst rob it of some taste of tediousness.
But fare thee well, there is a ducat for thee;
And, Launcelot, soon at supper shalt thou see
Lorenzo, who is thy new master's guest.
Give him this letter—do it secretly—
And so farewell. I would not have my father
See me in talk with thee.

Launcelot Adieu. Tears exhibit° my tongue, most beautiful pagan, most sweet Jew. If a Christian do not play the knave and get° thee, I am much deceived. But adieu. These foolish drops do something° drown my manly spirit. Adieu.

Jessica Farewell, good Launcelot. [Exit Launcelot.]
Alack, what heinous sin is it in me
To be ashamed to be my father's child.
But though I am a daughter to his blood,
I am not to his manners.° O Lorenzo,
If thou keep promise I shall end this strife,
Become a Christian and thy loving wife. Exit.

Scene iv Enter Gratiano, Lorenzo, Salerio, and Solanio.

Lorenzo Nay, we will slink away in suppertime,
Disguise us at my lodging, and return all in an hour.

Gratiano We have not made good preparation.

Salerio We have not spoke us° yet of torchbearers.

Scene iii

1-9 We find out the young woman on stage is Shylock's daughter, but she remains unnamed in this scene. Though well-educated, Jessica is mostly silent throughout the play.

The scene is in front of Shylock's door; and its rhythm partly informed with fearing discovery by him. She and Launcelot are leave-taking as friends: might he be carrying his worldly goods in a suitcase? Friendship is shown because they share vocabulary, for example the word 'hell'; and she entrusts to him a 'secret' letter. Gobbo has simply dropped out of the play.

blunder for "inhibit;" i.e. restrain

get hold of 2) get with child

somewhat

Jessica is sexually ripe and resourceful, making use of Launcelot as a go-between. Is she upset? Launcelot cries as he takes his leave but we learn she too may leave, and therefore can say 'fare thee well' in good heart .

10-20 Launcelot's extravagant compliment underlines the Jewish/Christian issue, while alerting us to his feelings. Is the jesting here a cover for real sadness? Note how his lingering 'adieus' have none of the bravado of 2.2.

1) character 2) customs

Jessica's next speech has five silent beats. Do they come after 'Farewell good Launcelot' as she wrestles with her conscience, articulating the breach to come between herself and her father? Her course of action is clear, though the strife within is not resolved.

Scene iv

1-8 We begin in mid-argument, in a public space. Lorenzo is insistent they go to the masque; Gratiano, Salerio and Solanio are equally resistant. As if to emphasise the rapidity of events Lorenzo mentions the time, and that he has moved lodgings. Has he moved lodgings because something is afoot with Jessica?

bespoken ourselves; i.e. ordered, or perhaps "discussed arrangements about" if "us" is an error for "as"

SOLANIO 'Tis vile unless it may be quaintly ordered,°
And better in my mind not undertook.

LORENZO 'Tis now but four of clock. We have two hours
To furnish us.°

Enter LAUNCELOT [with a letter.]

Friend Launcelot, what's the news?

LAUNCELOT And° it shall please you to break up° this [Presents the letter.], it shall seem to signify.°

LORENZO I know the hand;° in faith 'tis a fair hand,°
And whiter than the paper it writ on
Is the fair hand that writ.

GRATIANO Love-news, in faith.

LAUNCELOT By your leave, sir. [Starts to leave.]

LORENZO Whither goest thou?

LAUNCELOT Marry, sir, to bid my old master the Jew to sup tonight with my new master the Christian.

LORENZO Hold here, take this [Gives money.] Tell gentle Jessica
I will not fail her; speak it privately.

Exit [LAUNCELOT the] clown.

Go, gentlemen,
Will you prepare you for this masque tonight?
I am provided of° a torchbearer.

SALERIO Ay, marry, I'll be gone about it straight.

SOLANIO And so will I.

LORENZO Meet me and Gratiano
At Gratiano's lodging some° hour hence.

SALERIO 'Tis good we do so. Exeunt [SALERIO and SOLANIO.]

GRATIANO Was not that letter from fair Jessica?

LORENZO I must needs tell thee all. She hath directed
How I shall take her from her father's house,

is skilfully (or elegantly) managed

provide for ourselves

if unseal

will become known (Launcelot uses a pompous expression to try to sound dignified)

handwriting 11) beautiful writing 13) lovely hand

9-19 Launcelot arrives with the letter and becomes part of this rapid movement. Jessica has just asked Launcelot to deliver the letter at suppertime. Why does he deliver it now? To preen and show-off his new fools' livery and that he has a new master? Does Launcelot seek Lorenzo because, with Shylock invited, there will be little opportunity to give him Jessica's letter at dinner?

With the introduction of the letter the whole tone of the scene changes. Lorenzo's lines are a by-product of his reading the letter. The distraction leads to Gratiano's comment, 'Love-news in faith', loaded with sarcasm, irony or humour. Lorenzo asks him to give Jessica a token of faith as proof he has received her letter, and to 'speak it privately'. Launcelot leaves.

20-27 Lorenzo's tone has a new and persuasive authority. This time Gratiano doesn't lead a counter-attack.

with

about an

28-38 Lorenzo needs to tell Gratiano all. Is the news so joyous he has to share it? Or is he probing Gratiano's reaction to his running away with a Jewess?

What gold and jewels she is furnished with,
What page's suit she hath in readiness.°
If e'er the Jew her father come to heaven,
It will be for his gentle daughter's sake;
And never dare misfortune cross her foot,°
Unless she° do it under this excuse:
That she is issue to° a faithless° Jew.
Come, go with me; peruse this as thou goest.

[Gives GRATIANO the letter.]

Fair Jessica shall be my torchbearer. Exeunt.

Scene v Enter [SHYLOCK the] Jew and his man [LAUNCELOT GOBBO] that was the clown.°

SHYLOCK Well, thou shalt see, thy eyes shall be thy judge,
The difference of old Shylock and Bassanio—
[Calls.] What Jessica!—Thou shall not gormandize°
As thou hast done with me—what Jessica!—
And sleep and snore, and rend° apparel out—
Why Jessica, I say!

LAUNCELOT Why Jessica!

SHYLOCK Who bids thee call? I do not bid thee call.

LAUNCELOT Your worship was wont to tell me I could do nothing without bidding.

Enter JESSICA.

JESSICA Call you? What is your will?

SHYLOCK I am bid forth to supper, Jessica;
There are my keys. But wherefore should I go?
I am not bid for love. They flatter me.
But yet I'll go in hate, to feed upon
The prodigal Christian. Jessica, my girl,

i.e. as a disguise

path

i.e. misfortune

Jessica is the child of unbelieving (in the Christian faith)

i.e. Launcelot is no longer just a rustic bumpkin but now also Bassanio's professional fool (see note to II.ii.136). But a comma in the original phrasing ("man that was,) may indicate only that he is Shylock's former servant.

eat gluttonously

wear out clothing

Scene v

1-11 We are again in front of Shylock's house; the scene veers between verse and prose. As they approach, Shylock addresses Launcelot while shouting for Jessica. Jessica does not reply to her father's calls until Launcelot mimics him, speaking in verse and calling her himself. Jessica appears after Launcelot's call. Is this deliberate or accidental? Is she avoiding Shylock but needing to know Launcelot's news? Shylock turns on him and reasserts his authority by treating him as a servant.

12-40 Shylock gives Jessica instructions (insistently calling her by name), while debating if he should go out to supper with Bassanio. He appears to resolve his worries, but feeling unsettled and ill-at-ease, he goes back to the debate. Launcelot plays the fool, working hard to cajole Shylock from his

Look to my house. I am right loath° to go.
There is some ill a-brewing towards my rest,
For I did dream of money-bags tonight.°

LAUNCELOT I beseech you, sir, go; my young master doth expect your reproach°—

SHYLOCK So do I his.

LAUNCELOT —And they have conspired° together. I will not say you shall see a masque, but if you do, then it was not for nothing that my nose fell a-bleeding on Black Monday last at six o'clock i'th'morning, falling out that year on Ash Wednesday was four year in th'afternoon.°

SHYLOCK What, are there masques? Hear you me, Jessica,
Lock up my doors, and when you hear the drum
And the vile squealing of the wry-necked fife,°
Clamber not you up to the casements° then,
Nor thrust your head into the public street
To gaze on Christian fools with varnished faces,°
But stop my house's ears—I mean my casements.
Let not the sound of shallow foppery° enter
My sober house. By Jacob's staff° I swear
I have no mind of feasting forth tonight,
But I will go. [To LAUNCELOT.] Go you before me, sirrah,
Say I will come.

LAUNCELOT I will go before, sir.
[Aside to JESSICA.] Mistress, look out at window for all this,°
There will come a Christian by,
Will be worth a Jewes' eye. [Exit LAUNCELOT.]

SHYLOCK What says that fool of Hagar's offspring,° ha?

JESSICA His words were "farewell mistress," nothing else.

SHYLOCK The patch° is kind enough, but a huge feeder,
Snail-slow in profit, and he sleeps by day
More than the wildcat.° Drones hive not with me,
Therefore I part with him, and part with him
To one that I would have him help to waste
His borrowed purse. Well, Jessica, go in.
Perhaps I will return immediately.

very reluctant

i.e. last night

Launcelot's blunder for "approach;" Shylock then makes a grim joke on the mistaken word

the (probably unintended) sinister sense hints at Lorenzo's scheme to elope with Jessica; Jessica may show fear that Shylock will suspect something

nonsensical omens of disaster mocking Shylock's fears and dreams

musician twisting his neck to play the fife, or "tuneless fife-player"

windows in metal hinged frames (whose open position on the side of a house Shylock compares to ears at l.34)

wearing painted masks

foolery

a symbol of heaven-sent "thrift:" Jacob set out to Padam-aran with only his staff and returned a rich man (Genesis 28:2, 32:10)

despite all that Shylock has said

Hagar (an Egyptian servant) and her son Ishmael were gentiles cast out by Abraham (Genesis 21:9-21)

fool

which is a nocturnal animal

frame of mind and get him to go. Why is he working so hard? Does he know Jessica will run away tonight? Is this why he was determined to run away from Shylock's house in the first place (2.1)? Is he trying to please his new master by not disappointing him? He lowers the temperature through humour, and goes into prose.

Shylock is worried because 'Christian fools' are out masquing. In the Peter Hall Company production with Dustin Hoffman's Shylock, "A genuine intimacy is shown by Shylock's tenderly paternal, back-rubbing embrace as he issues his directions. But this love is clearly something which his hatred of Christians can unbalance and get the better of, since it only takes news of the forthcoming masque for him to begin to shake her in rough, paranoid agitation, and Buller's [Jessica] stricken face lets you see the way her emotions shift between guilt at her imminent defection, love of her father and rebellious dread of him: (The Independent, 1989).

Now that Launcelot is gone he is afraid of leaving a sexually ripe daughter. The way the silent Jessica holds herself makes him feel she will obey, and he decides to go.

41-43 Yet Launcelot still has to give Lorenzo's something to Jessica, and given that Shylock is onstage, there has to be a certain distance between the two and him. There are a number of staging solutions: Launcelot and Shylock are in the street and when Jessica enters she stays at the door. Launcelot can then go to Jessica, leaving Shylock alone. Shylock can separate himself, come downstage when debating whether to supper or not. Or Jessica manoeuvres a distance apart so Launcelot can relay it as he passes by when leaving. Launcelot exits with a cryptic couplet.

44-55 Shylock's suspicions are clearly aroused. Did he get rid of Launcelot because he was afraid Launcelot might bed her? or act as a go-between? Does Shylock allow himself a moment of sentiment? or seeing how upset Jessica is, does he play act for her? He immediately tries to convince Jessica that he was right to let Launcelot go, thinking that's why she's upset.

What does Jessica do during Shylock's speech? Perhaps she is fighting to suppress joy, worry, and all her other emotions to keep them them hidden from Shylock. Perhaps she is ashamed,

Do as I bid you, shut doors after you.
Fast bind, fast find:°
A proverb never stale in thrifty mind. Exit.

JESSICA Farewell, and if my fortune be not crossed,
I have a father, you a daughter, lost. Exit.

Scene vi Enter the MASQUERS, GRATIANO, and SALERIO [with torchbearers.]

GRATIANO This is the penthouse° under which Lorenzo
Desired us to make stand.

SALERIO His hour is almost past.

GRATIANO And it is marvel° he out-dwells° his hour,
For lovers ever run before° the clock.

SALERIO O, ten times faster Venus' pigeons° fly
To seal Jove's bonds new made, than they are wont
To keep obliged faith unforfeited.°

GRATIANO That ever holds. Who riseth from a feast
With that keen appetite that he sits down?
Where is the horse that doth untread° again
His tedious measures° with the unbated° fire
That he did pace them first? All things that are
Are with more spirit chased than enjoyed.
How like a younger° or a prodigal
The scarfed bark° puts from her native bay,
Hugged and embraced by the strumpet° wind.
How like the prodigal doth she return
With over-weathered ribs° and ragged sails,
Lean, rent,° and beggared° by the strumpet wind.

Enter LORENZO.

SALERIO Here comes Lorenzo. More of this hereafter.

knowing she is about to run away, yet not saying goodbye to her father. He has to order her to go in, as if she's preoccupied.

i.e. that which is well secured is found safe

Shylock's split focus on the way he both trusts and distrusts Launcelot, Bassanio and Jessica, culminates in line 52, when he threatens to come home unexpectedly. That he has to repeat his instruction indicates Jessica's reluctance to go in.

56-57 When he is gone, she re-opens the door and says 'Farewell' after him. She sees Shylock for the last time.

Scene vi

projecting roof or upper storey of a house (in the theatre the stage balcony or gallery)

1-19 Until Lorenzo enters, this scene is about waiting. Gratiano and Salerio enter in the dark, masked and with lit torches. They are just in time to meet Lorenzo in front of Shylock's house. Yet no-one is there. Their conversation about lovers being last is a way of passing the time, waiting. Underlying the stories is the question: what has happened to Lorenzo? Throughout the telling, Gratiano and Salerio must be looking out for him.

astonishing overruns

ahead of

the doves that drew Venus' chariot, or "lovers"

pledged (in marriage), unbroken

retrace

paces keen

younger son, as in the parable of the Prodigal son (Luke 15) which informs Gratiano's metaphor of a sea venture

ship decorated with streamers

harlot; i.e. variable (alluding to the harlots on whom the Prodigal son wasted his fortune)

timbers

torn ravaged and impoverished

20-32 When Lorenzo enters he's courteous, in a hurry, and doesn't let them answer. Jessica enters

LORENZO Sweet friends, your patience for my long abode.°
Not I but my affairs have made you wait.
When you shall please to play the thieves for wives
I'll watch as long for you therein. Approach,
Here dwells my father° Jew. Ho, who's within?

[Enter] JESSICA above [in boy's clothes.]

JESSICA Who are you? Tell me for more certainty,
Albeit I'll swear that I do know your tongue.

LORENZO Lorenzo, and thy love.

JESSICA Lorenzo certain, and my love indeed,
For who love I so much? And now who knows
But you, Lorenzo, whether I am yours?

LORENZO Heaven and thy thoughts are witness that thou art.

JESSICA Here catch this casket, it is worth the pains.
I am glad 'tis night, you do not look on me,
For I am much ashamed of my exchange.°
But love is blind, and lovers cannot see
The pretty follies that themselves commit,
For if they could, Cupid himself would blush
To see me thus transformed to a boy.

LORENZO Descend, for you must be my torchbearer.

JESSICA What, must I hold a candle to my shames?
They in themselves, good sooth, are too too light.°
Why, 'tis an office of discovery,° love,
And I should be obscured.°

LORENZO So are you, sweet,
Even in the lovely garnish° of a boy.
But come at once,
For the close° night doth play the runaway,°
And we are stayed for° at Bassiano's feast.

JESSICA I will make fast the doors and gild° myself
With some more ducats, and be with you straight.

[Exit above.]

delay

'above', dressed in boy's clothing. Being in the dark and the masquers dressed up, she has to ask who they are. There is no immediate reply. Is Jessica worried about Lorenzo's commitment to her? Lorenzo reassures her.

father-in-law; Lorenzo is presumptuous and/or sarcastic

33-50 She throws down a 'casket' of money and jewels, reminding us of Portia's caskets. Yet she delays coming down. Is she ashamed of exchanging her dress for a suit? her father for a lover? Jewishness for Christianity? Lorenzo has to remind her to act and yet Jessica procrastinates. Is she afraid of going out into society? Lorenzo interrupts her more assertively, and her long silence forces him to continue to persuade her. She is so wired, she steals yet more money.

disguise

clear, with a pun on the sense "immodest"

i.e. the torchbearer's function to reveal things

hidden

apparel

secret i.e. is quickly passing

expected

stock up

GRATIANO Now by my hood, a gentle° and no Jew.

LORENZO Beshrew° me but I love her heartily,
For she is wise, if I can judge of her,
And fair she is, if that mine eyes be true,
And true she is, as she hath proved herself,
And therefore like herself, wise, fair and true,
Shall she be placed in my constant soul.

Enter JESSICA.

What, art thou come? On, gentlemen, away,
Our masking mates by this time for us stay.

Exit [LORENZO with JESSICA, SALERIO (and TORCHBEARERS); GRATIANO stays behind.]

Enter ANTONIO.

ANTONIO Who's there?

GRATIANO Signor Antonio?°

ANTONIO Fie, fie, Gratiano, where are all the rest?
'Tis nine o'clock, our friends all stay for you.
No masque tonight, the wind is come about;
Bassanio presently° will go aboard.
I have sent twenty out to seek for you.

GRATIANO I am glad on't. I desire no more delight
Than to be under sail and gone tonight. Exeunt.

Scene vii [Flourish of cornets.] Enter PORTIA with [the Prince of] MOROCCO and both their trains.

PORTIA Go, draw aside the curtains and discover°
The several caskets to this noble prince.

[The curtains are drawn.]

Now make your choice.

refined woman (again with a pun on "gentile")

literally "curse," but Lorenzo uses the word jubilantly

51-58 Lines 51-57 are partly there to give Jessica time to come down, while building expectations in the masquers. Jim Hiley says of Peter Hall's production: "There's a nice moment when Lorenzo declares, 'Beshrew me, but I love her heartily', while groping the casket of jewels hoisted down by Jessica" (The Listener, 1989).

Jessica's entrance makes Lorenzo lose all sense of what he's saying. Is it the awkwardness of two lovers meeting for the first time? Or the publicness of their first meeting? Is there a sexual charge in her being dressed as a boy? Does Lorenzo throw her a torch? Is 'on gentlemen, away' affectionate teasing?

59-67 Antonio's 'who's there?' reminds the audience that it is dark, but also that Gratiano needs to remove his mask. Antonio blurts out his message as if out of breath, indicating the urgency for Gratiano to catch Bassanio's boat. It's odd that Antonio looks for Gratiano. Why? Is it so the audience sees that Antonio knows nothing of Jessica's and Lorenzo's running away?

After the torchbearers' departure, the scene may darken

immediately

Scene vii

reveal

1-3 The scene takes us to Belmont, to the casket room. This time they are revealed or brought on. Whatever Portia's self-doubt in 1.2, she commands this scene—it's business: open the curtain and choose.

Morocco This first of gold, who this inscription bears,
"Who chooseth me shall gain what many men desire."
The second silver, which this promise carries,
"Who chooseth me shall get as much as he deserves."
This third, dull lead, with warning all as blunt,°
"Who chooseth me must give and hazard all he hath."
How shall I know if I do choose the right?

Portia The one of them contains my picture, Prince;
If you choose that, then I am yours withal.°

Morocco Some god direct my judgement. Let me see,
I will survey th'inscriptions back again.
What says this leaden casket?
"Who chooseth me must give and hazard all he hath."
Must give, for what? For lead, hazard for lead?
This casket threatens. Men that hazard all
Do it in hope of fair advantages;°
A golden mind stoops not to shows of dross;°
I'll then nor give nor hazard aught for lead.
What says the silver with her virgin hue?
"Who chooseth me shall get as much as he deserves."
As much as he deserves; pause there, Morocco,
And weigh thy value with an even hand.°
If thou be'st rated by thy estimation°
Thou dost deserve enough, and yet enough
May not extend so far as to the lady;
And yet to be afeard of my deserving
Were but a weak disabling° of myself.
As much as I deserve—why, that's the lady.
I do in birth deserve her, and in fortunes,
And in graces, and in qualities of breeding;
But more than these, in love I do deserve.
What if I strayed no farther, but chose here?
Let's see once more this saying graved in gold.
"Who chooseth me shall gain what many men desire."
Why, that's the lady; all the world desires her.
From the four corners of the earth they come
To kiss this shrine, this mortal breathing saint.
The Hyrcanian° deserts and the vasty wilds
Of wide Arabia are as throughfares now

4-12 Morocco sees the gold one first, and it may be that during dinner Portia and Nerissa have guessed his likes and so have arranged the caskets in such a way (by lights, placement, the way they dress: does Nerissa stand by one?) that he will choose a contrary one.

1) abrupt 2) lusterless (as lead)

1) when it is done 2) with all I own

13-34 Morocco reads and re-reads the inscriptions, first going up the line of caskets and then back down again. Does he 'delay'? Is he looking for inspiration? Both would build tension. Note how Morocco's language is about himself; he makes no connections between Portia and the caskets.

Morocco will not gamble for lead, so he moves to silver. He dwells on it twice as long, and for the first time we sense some hesitation (l.3.1), though this doubt is mainly about losing face.

gains

worthless matter (literally the scum produced refining metals)

impartially

reputation

underrating

35-46 By line 35 he increases the tension by threatening to choose—but then goes to gold and again doubles the time he spends on that casket. Morocco gets carried away by his own oratory while also fishing for help from Portia (ll.43,47,48), who remains silent. Is this why he chooses not to choose?

area south of the Caspian sea famous for its wildness

For princes to come view fair Portia.
The watery kingdom,° whose ambitious head
Spits in the face of heaven, is no bar
To stop the foreign spirits,° but they come
As o'er a brook to see fair Portia.
One of these three contains her heavenly picture.
Is't like that lead contains her? 'Twere damnation
To think so base a thought; it were too° gross
To rib her cerecloth in the obscure grave.°
Or shall I think in silver she's immured,
Being ten times undervalued to tried° gold?
O sinful thought! Never so rich a jem
Was set in worse than gold. They have in England
A coin that bears the figure of an angel
Stamped in gold—but that's insculped upon;°
But here an angel in a golden bed
Lies all within. Deliver me the key;
Here do I choose, and thrive as I may.

PORTIA There take it, Prince, and if my form° lie there,
Then I am yours.

MOROCCO [Opens the gold casket.] O hell! What have we here?
A carrion° death, within whose empty eye
There is a written scroll. I'll read the writing.
All that glisters is not gold,
Often have you heard that told;
Many a man his life hath sold
But° my outside to behold;
Gilded tombs do worms enfold.
Had you been as wise as bold,
Young in limbs, in judgement old,
Your answer had not been inscrolled.°
Fare you well, your suit is cold.
Cold indeed, and labor lost;
Then farewell heat, and welcome frost.
Portia, adieu; I have too grieved a heart
To take a tedious leave. Thus losers part.

Exit [MOROCCO with his train; flourish of cornets.]

PORTIA A gentle riddance. Draw the curtains, go.

the seas, ruled by Neptune

men of courage

47-60 He speeds up (the gold casket got 22 lines, now all three are given 11), and in thrall to his own words chooses gold.

even more

enclose her burial shroud in such an illustrious grave (corpses of upper-class people were normally encased in lead)

purified

merely engraved on the surface

image

61-78 Portia must have given him the key to the gold casket by line 63 since Morocco is already reacting to its contents. With 'A carrion Death' he might pick the skull out of the casket, and take out the scroll stuck through one of the eye sockets. The nine-line poem has one rhyme. Is this merely playful? incantatory?

Morocco extends the enscrolled poem by concluding with a couplet of his own. Does he put the scroll and skull back into the casket during these lines?

death's head, skull

only

written on this scroll; i.e. you would have received a better answer had you chosen differently

79-80 Portia's 'a gentle riddance' is a relief, and

[Curtains are drawn.]
Let all of his complexion° choose me so. Exeunt.

Scene viii Enter SALERIO and SOLANIO.

SALERIO Why, man, I saw Bassanio under sail,
With him is Gratiano gone along,
And in their ship I am sure Lorenzo is not.

SOLANIO The villain Jew with outcries raised° the Duke,
Who went with him to search Bassanio's ship.

SALERIO He came too late, the ship was under sail;
But there the Duke was given to understand
That in a gondola were seen together
Lorenzo and his amorous Jessica.°
Besides, Antonio certified° the Duke
They were not with Bassanio in his ship.

SOLANIO I never heard a passion° so confused,
So strange, outrageous and so variable
As the dog Jew did utter in the streets:
"My daughter! O my ducats! O my daughter!
Fled with a Christian! O my Christian ducats!
Justice! The law! My ducats and my daughter!
A sealed bag, two sealed bags of ducats
Of double ducats, stolen from me by my daughter!
And jewels, two stones, two rich and precious stones,
Stolen by my daughter! Justice! Find the girl,
She hath the stones upon her and the ducats!"

SALERIO Why, all the boys in Venice follow him
Crying his stones°, his daughter, and his ducats.

SOLANIO Let good Antonio look he keep his day
Or he shall pay for this.

SALERIO Marry, well remembered.
I reasoned° with a Frenchman yesterday,

the audience can hear her distaste for Morocco's 'complexion'. Is it a racist remark? or a comment on his character?

1) temperament 2) skin color.

Scene viii

1-25 We are in a public space and have yet to learn Salerio's and Solanio's names. Do they serve a choral function in furthering the narrative? Shylock is inconsolable and outraged at the loss of daughter and money, and though neither Bassanio nor Antonio have anything to do with it, he goes to search Bassanio's ship.

roused

What is the dramatic tension between Salerio and Solanio? Is it that both only know part of the story? and each needs to fill the other in? How do we 'play the anti-semitism'? Salerio and Solanio are gleeful about Shylock's discomfort. They, especially Solanio, talk about him using Antonio's abusive language.

apparently a false report to cover Lorenzo and Jessica's trail

assured

passionate outburst

Lines 15-22 quote Shylock, but his words and confusions are shaped by Solanio. Solanio dwells on daughter and ducats, on sexual jokes: jewels, stones and balls. Is this the sexual challenge of a daughter who runs away from her father? or merely a joke about fathers and daughters? Is it racism? Salerio says 'all the boys in Venice follow him': is Shylock still crying in the streets? Is Salerio's and Solanio's reporting before the event has finished?

the boys' jeers pun on the sense "testicles"

26-53 The subject changes to Antonio's ship sinking. The play has so far observed the unity of time and action. Has Salerio thereore had this information when they first met Antonio in 1.1?

spoke

Does the detail Solanio uses for Antonio's

Who told me, in the narrow seas° that part
The French and English, there miscarried
A vessel of our country richly fraught.°
I thought upon Antonio when he told me
And wished in silence that it were not his.

SOLANIO You were best to tell Antonio what you hear,
Yet do not suddenly, for it may grieve him.

SALERIO A kinder gentleman treads not the earth.
I saw Bassanio and Antonio part:
Bassanio told him he would make some speed
Of his return; he answered "Do not so.
Slubber not° business for my sake, Bassanio,
But stay the very riping of the time,°
And for the Jew's bond which he hath of me,
Let it not enter in your mind of° love.
Be merry, and employ your chiefest thoughts
To courtship and such fair ostents° of love
As shall conveniently° become you there."
And even there, his eye big with tears,
Turning his face, he put his hand behind him
And with affection wondrous sensible°
He wrung Bassanio's hand, and so they parted.

SOLANIO I think he only loves the world for him.°
I pray thee let us go and find him out
And quicken° his embraced heaviness
With some delight or other.

SALERIO Do we so. Exeunt.

Scene ix Enter NERISSA and a SERVITOR.°

NERISSA Quick, quick, I pray thee, draw the curtain straight.°

[Servitor draws the curtains.]

The Prince of Aragon hath ta'en his oath
And comes to his election presently.°

i.e. the English channel

laden

leave-taking suggest that he desires Antonio? Antonio is proactive and Bassanio wordless: Solanio comments 'I think he only loves the world for him'. Is this the reason for Antonio's melancholy? Does it help build a picture of an erotic relationship?

Their mocking of, and cruelty to Shylock is balanced by their sensitivity and love for Antonio. Do the constructs of their language begin to set up the confrontation between Antonio and Shylock?

don't hurry over

until your business is fully completed

thoughts or intentions about

displays

properly

palpably evident, strongly felt

i.e. is all he lives for

dispell the sadness he has clung to

servant

Scene ix

at once

1-3 Back in Belmont, the curtains are pulled, the caskets put on display as Aragon enters with his train. Does Portia enter with hers? If she's alone, does it suggest that there has not been enough time to assemble her train?

choice straight away

[Flourish of cornets.] Enter [the Prince of] ARAGON, his train, and PORTIA.

PORTIA Behold, there stand the caskets, noble Prince.
If you choose that wherein I am contained,
Straight shall our nuptial rites be solemnized;
But if you fail, without more speech, my lord,
You must be gone from hence immediately.

ARAGON I am enjoined by oath to observe three things:
First, never to unfold to anyone
Which casket 'twas I chose; next, if I fail
Of the right casket, never in my life
To woo a maid in way of marriage;
Lastly, if I do fail in fortune of my choice,
Immediately to leave you and be gone.

PORTIA To these injunctions everyone doth swear
That comes to hazard for my worthless self.

ARAGON And so have I addressed me.° Fortune now
To my heart's hope! Gold, silver, and base lead.
"Who chooseth me must give and hazard all he hath."
You shall look fairer ere I give or hazard.
What says the golden chest? Ha, let me see:
"Who chooseth me shall gain what many men desire."
What many men desire; that "many" may be meant
By the fool multitude that choose by° show,
Not learning more than the fond° eye doth teach,
Which pries not to th'interior, but like the martlet°
Builds in the weather on the outward wall,°
Even in the force and road of casuality.°
I will not choose what many men desire,
Because I will not jump with° common spirits
And rank me with the barbarous multitudes.
Why then, to thee thou silver treasure house,
Tell me once more what title thou dost bear:
"Who chooseth me shall get as much as he deserves."
And well said too; for who shall go about
To cozen° fortune and be honorable
Without the stamp° of merit. Let none presume
To wear an undeserved dignity.

4-18 Portia gets down to business. Does her repetition of instructions help us understand why her little body is 'aweary'?

More information about the terms and condition of choosing is given, to which Aragon assents. Have Nerissa and Portia had time to work out Aragon's likely choice? might they do so from the reference to his name? Are they wearing silver dresses?

prepared myself (by swearing to these conditions)

19-49 It took Morocco five lines to dismiss lead, yet Aragon dismisses it in one. He overlooks silver and swiftly moves to gold. Why? Has he already read the inscriptions on the caskets while Portia was reciting the conditions? Does Aragon play the soldier to appear decisive? Has Belmont been reacting to his pace? He dismisses gold as 'show'. When he moves on to silver, it's as if he's eliminated the other two. Line 34 confirms he has read the inscriptions. The time he spends on the silver casket is double that of gold.

Neither Aragon nor Morocco think through the implication of the caskets. Morocco was carried away by his oratory and Aragon gets trapped by his logic of elimination. They are opposites: Aragon is fixated on class, he doesn't relate to people, and never shows desire for Portia; Morocco is all vanity, a womaniser who lusts for her.

refer to

foolish

swift (but here probably "house-martin")

exposed to the weather on the outside (often most attractive-looking) wall

power and path of misfortune

follow after

cheat

entitlement

O that estates, degrees,° and offices
Were not derived corruptly, and that clear honor
Were purchased by the merit of the wearer.
How many then should cover that stand bare?°
How many be commanded that command?
How much low peasantry would then be gleaned°
From the true seed of honor? And how much honor°
Picked from the chaff and ruin° of the times
To be new varnished?° Well, but to my choice:
"Who chooseth me shall get as much as he deserves."
I will assume desert. Give me a key for this,
And instantly unlock my fortunes here.

[Opens the silver casket.]

PORTIA Too long a pause for that which you find there.

ARAGON What's here? The portrait of a blinking idiot°
Presenting me a schedule.° I will read it—
How much unlike art thou to Portia.
How much unlike my hopes and my deservings.
"Who chooseth me shall have as much as he deserves"?
Did I deserve no more than a fool's head?
Is that my prize? Are my deserts no better?

PORTIA To offend and judge are distinct offices,
And of opposed natures.°

ARAGON What is here?
[Reads.] The fire seven times tried this;°
Seven times tried that judgement is
That did never choose amiss.
Some there be that shadows kiss,
Such have but a shadow's bliss.
There be fools alive, iwis,°
Silvered o'er,° and so was this.
Take what wife you will to bed,
I will ever be your head;°
So be gone, you are sped.°
Still° more fool I shall appear
By the time I linger here.
With one fool's head I came to woo,
But I go away with two.

status and/or property, social rank

keep their hats on rather than doffing them (out of respect to superiors); i.e. be masters not servants

culled and discarded

rightful inheritors of nobility

1) refuse 2) those made destitute

regain their illustrious standing

50-61 While the repetition of the scene emphasises the strain on Portia, speed is needed because the audience knows Bassanio is on his way. Aragon quickly unlocks the casket and takes out the portrait with its message. For the first time he delays, trying to understand what has gone wrong.

some stage productions have Aragon looking into a mirror rather than at a jester's head

written scroll

i.e. it's not for me to say

purified this; i.e. the silver of the casket

62-77 There is a viciousness in the way the scroll makes Aragon the fool. He stays within the seven-beat line of the message until he leaves, even mimicking the rhyme. Is Aragon doing this to save face?—he can do what it does? His leave-taking is swift and correct, if bitter.

certainly

white-haired and thus appearing wise

i.e. you will always have a fool's head

you've had it!

even

Sweet, adieu. I'll keep my oath,
Patiently to bear my wroth.° [Exit ARAGON with his train.]

PORTIA Thus hath the candle singed the moth.
O these deliberate° fools, when they do choose,
They have the wisdom by their wit to lose!°

NERISSA The ancient saying is no heresy:
Hanging and wiring goes by destiny.

PORTIA Come draw the curtain, Nerissa.

[NERISSA draws the curtain.]

Enter [a] MESSENGER.

MESSENGER Where is my lady?

PORTIA Here, what would my lord?°

MESSENGER Madam, there is alighted at your gate
A young Venetian, one that comes before
To signify th'approaching of his lord,
From whom he bringeth sensible regreets;°
To wit, besides commends° and courteous breath,°
Gifts of rich value. Yet° I have not seen
So likely° an ambassador of love.
A day in April never came so sweet
To show how costly° summer was at hand,
As this fore-spurrer° comes before his lord.

PORTIA No more I pray thee, I am half afeard
Thou wilt say anon he is some kin to thee,
Thou spend'st such high-day° wit in praising him.
Come, come, Nerissa, for I long to see
Quick Cupid's post° that comes so mannerly.°

NERISSA Bassanio, Lord Love,° if thy will it be! Exeunt.

calamity

rational

to fail by trusting reasoning alone

Portia responds with a jest to "my lady"

1) strongly felt greetings 2) presents

commendations speech

Until now

promising

abundant

forerunner, herald

holiday; i.e. uncommon

messenger in such a becoming way

i.e. Cupid

78-100 Portia is constant, the finality of her rhyming couplet shows she has no pity. The scene appears to close with a pair of rhyming couplets suggesting it will end the same way as 2.1, but unexpectedly continues, relaxing into prose, by joking to and fro with 'lord' and 'lady' between Portia and the messenger. For the first time we get a detailed description of the arrival of a suitor. The messenger is fulsome and animated, and we are alerted to a change in the atmosphere.

Is Gratiano the ambassador of love who comes knocking at the door? Would a messenger be such an ambassador unless he too came wooing? Portia's response is half-mocking, as if alarmed at the messenger's unusual tone. She becomes almost giddy. When Nerissa names Bassanio aloud, she expresses what Portia half fears. Does Nerissa also express her hopes? For the first time, the tone of the play changes to one of anticipation, hope and excitement. We are about to go into a romantic comedy.

ACT III

Scene i [Enter] SOLANIO and SALERIO.

SOLANIO Now what news on the Rialto?

SALERIO Why, yet it lives there unchecked° that Antonio hath a ship of rich lading wrecked on the narrow seas°—the Goodwins° I think they call the place, a very dangerous flat, and fatal, where the carcasses of many a tall ship lie buried, as they say, if my gossip Report° be an honest woman of her word.

SOLANIO I would she were as lying a gossip in that as ever knapped° ginger or made her neighbors believe she wept for the death of a third husband. But it is true, without any slips of prolixity° or crossing the plain highway of talk,° that the good Antonio, the honest Antonio—O that I had title good enough to keep his name company—

SALERIO Come, the full stop.°

SOLANIO Ha, what sayest thou? Why, the end is, he hath a ship lost.

SALERIO I would it might prove the end of his losses.

Enter SHYLOCK.

SOLANIO Let me say amen betimes,° lest the devil cross my prayer, for here he comes in the likeness of a Jew. How now, Shylock, what news among the merchants?

SHYLOCK You knew, none so well, none so well as you, of my daughter's flight.

SALERIO That's certain. I for my part knew the tailor that made the wings° she flew withal.

ACT III. Scene i

is talked about there uncontradicted

English channel

Goodwin Sands, a shoal or "flat" off the coast of Kent

old confidante Rumor

nibbled (ginger was associated with old women)

lapses into longwinded talk diverging from plain speech

come to the point

1-15 The scene is in a public place. We are still unaware of Salerio's and Solanio's names, though their concerns are continuous: Antonio's sea ventures, and meeting up with him. 'Now' indicates time has passed and there is additional news, though the wreck they speak of is the same as before. Is the purpose of the scene to build a picture of Antonio's mounting losses? Is its dramatic purpose to show how Salerio's earlier conjecture is becoming public rumour?

Solanio asks for news from the Rialto but witholds his own. As he speaks he becomes distressed with the repetition of Antonio's name. If it's only rumour, why are they worried? Does rumour gain currency if repeated enough? Does not seeing Antonio add to this sense of disquiet? Do they know of the bond?

before it's too late

i.e. the boy's clothes Jessica used as a disguise, although "tailor" may refer figuratively to Lorenzo

16-34 Just as they speak of Antonio's 'losses' they are interrupted by Shylock's entrance. Shylock has been called 'devil', 'Jew', 'a dog', but in this scene, unusually, he is called by his name? Why?

Solanio asks for news from the Rialto, but Shylock is more concerned about his daughter. Does he see them? or walk past them deliberately. They call out. Shylock pressures them by pointing out they were at dinner with Lorenzo, himself and others.

Salerio confesses knowing the tailor who made Jessica's boy's clothes. Clearly the escape was well-planned, lending credibility to Shylock's suspicion that everyone, including Bassanio and Antonio, are involved. Salerio and Solanio try to con-

SOLANIO And Shylock for his own part knew the bird was fledge,° and then it is the complexion° of them all to leave the dam.°

SHYLOCK She is damned for it.

SALERIO That's certain, if the devil may be her judge.

SHYLOCK My own flesh and blood to rebel.

SOLANIO Out upon it, old carrion,° rebels it at these years?°

SHYLOCK I say my daughter is my flesh and my blood.

SALERIO There is more difference between thy flesh and hers than between jet° and ivory, more between your bloods than there is between red° wine and Rhenish.° But tell us, do you hear whether Antonio have had any loss at sea or no?

SHYLOCK There I have another bad match: a bankrupt, a prodigal who dare scarce show his head upon the Rialto, a beggar that was used to come so smug° upon the mart.° Let him look to his bond. He was wont to call me usurer, let him look to his bond. He was wont to lend money for a Christian courtesy, let him look to his bond.

SALERIO Why, I am sure if he forfeit, thou wilt not take his flesh. What's that good for?

SHYLOCK To bait fish withal.° If it will feed nothing else, it will feed my revenge. He hath disgraced me and hindered me half a million, laughed at my losses, mocked at my gains, scorned my nation, thwarted my bargains, cooled my friends, heated mine enemies, and what's his reason? I am a Jew. Hath not a Jew eyes? Hath not a Jew hands, organs, dimensions,° senses, affections, passions? Fed with the same food, hurt with the same weapons, subject to the same diseases, healed by the same means, warmed and cooled by the same winter and summer as a Christian is? If you prick us do we not bleed? If you tickle us do we not laugh? If you poison us do we not die? And if you wrong us shall we not revenge? If we are like you in the rest, we will resemble you in that. If a Jew wrong a Christian, what is his humility?° Revenge. If a Christian wrong a Jew, what should his sufferance° be by Christian example? Why, revenge! The villainy you teach

ready to fly natural inclination

mother

vince Shylock that Jessica was ready to leave, and become exasperated by his incomprehension. Salerio, who has not made an antisemitic remark, deals with him head-on: Jessica and Shylock are as different as black and white, or red wine and white. There was no conspiracy, Jessica won't be back as a daughter or a Jewess.

living corpse Solanio deliberately misinterprets Shylock's cry about his "flesh and blood": "Can you still be sexually aroused at your age?"

black marble or lignite

i.e. common table Rhine wine

35-61 The two men again press Shylock for news from the Rialto. Is it to confirm rumour? to check what Shylock knows? Shylock, deeply hurt and upset, focuses his emotional energy on Antonio. Both his daughter and Antonio are 'bad matches'. He describes Antonio as 'ruined', a 'beggar', and as he mentions the bond, is his response sharpened by the conspiracy he senses around Jessica's running away? When Salerio tries to reason with him, he pushes his hatred further, saying he'll have Antonio's flesh to bait fish with.

smoothly and/or in a self-satisfied way the market-place

As Shylock's speech pours out over Antonio, and by proxy Solanio and Salerio, the discrepancy between the action here and the mocking tone of his 'fevered pitch' at 2.8.12-22 becomes overwhelming. Has Shylock chosen to move outside the bounds of acceptable behaviour? He is en-raged.

with it

Solanio and Salerio may be transfixed by his hatred but they also need to listen to inform Antonio. Indeed, is the earlier part of the scene a taunting of Shylock into this intemperate response? In Antony Sher's performance for the RSC "He is chased across the stage before being viciously battered and rises bloodied but unbowed to succumb to rage and grief. 'The villainy you teach me I will execute' becomes the key line of this production" (The Guardian, 1988).

bodily proportions

i.e. the Christian's response to his injury (which should be guided by Christian precept of humility)

i.e. the Jew's self-restraint

me I will execute, and it shall go hard but I will better the instruction.

Enter a MAN from ANTONIO.

MAN [To SOLANIO and SALERIO.] Gentlemen, my master Antonio is at his house and desires to speak with you both.

SALERIO We have been up and down to seek him.

Enter TUBAL.

SOLANIO Here comes another of the tribe. A third cannot be matched° unless the devil himself turn Jew.

Exeunt gentlemen [SOLANIO, SALERIO, and ANTONIO'S MAN.]

SHYLOCK How now, Tubal, what news from Genoa? Hast thou found my daughter?

TUBAL I often came where I did hear of her, but cannot find her.

SHYLOCK Why, there, there, there, there. A diamond gone cost me two thousand ducats in Frankfurt. The curse never fell upon our nation till now, I never felt it till now. Two thousand ducats in that, and other precious, precious jewels. I would my daughter were dead at my foot and the jewels in her ear. Would she were hearsed° at my foot and the ducats in her coffin! No news of them? Why, so—and I know not what's spent in the search. Why thou° loss upon loss, the thief gone with so much, and so much to find the thief, and no satisfaction, no revenge, nor no ill luck stirring but what lights o' my shoulders, no sighs but o' my breathing, no tears but o' my shedding.

TUBAL Yes, other men have ill luck too. Antonio, as I heard in Genoa—

SHYLOCK What, what, what? Ill luck, ill luck?

TUBAL —hath an argosy cast away° coming from Tripolis.

SHYLOCK I thank God, I thank God! Is it true, Is it true?

TUBAL I spoke with some of the sailors that escaped the wreck.

SHYLOCK I thank thee, good Tubal, good news, good news! Ha, ha!

62-66 Antonio's man enters to say he is at home. Does this help build the atmosphere that something is amiss? So far, Antonio has only been seen in public places even when most melancholic, yet now he wants Salerio and Solanio to come to his house? We know they are not intimates. So why? Salerio underlines this when he says they have looked for him everywhere, (though they do not feel free to go to his house).

Hard on the servant's heels comes Tubal. The atmosphere completely alters and Solanio's racist jibes re-emerge. In many productions Solanio spits in Tubal's face. In Gregory Doran's production for the RSC June Treadwell comments "When he [Shylock] wipes the Christian spit off Tubal's face, he reveals a humanity and dignity he would never bother to show his tormentors, or to his daughter" (The Spectator, 1997).

i.e. found to match them

67-80 It's only in lines 72-3 that we understand several days must have passed since Jessica ran away. For Shylock to sustain his anger over this time suggests its deep-rootedness. Portia's father gives her away from the grave; but Shylock, alive, is denied the same right.

Tubal's information that Jessica was often spoken about suggests they are spending a great deal of money. Shylock's language begins to spin out of control. His grieving vacillates between money and daughter. Antonio has ships and Bassanio, while Shylock has money and Jessica.

coffined

To Dustin Hoffman's understated Shylock, David Nathan observes: "The key to Hoffman's performance comes when, after his daughter has run away, he tells Tubal: 'The curse never fell upon our nation until now.' Tubal looks at him as if to ask 'What kind of world have you been living in?' and Shylock quickly responds 'I,' he stresses, 'never felt it until now.'" (Jewish Chronicle, 1989). When Olivier's Shylock heard about Antonio's misfortunes he broke into an exultant little dance.

Shylock apparently addresses "loss"

Shylock's reaction is so extreme that he swings between grieving for a daughter to treating her as a dead whore. He associates jewels with 'balls', hears'd with arsed, foot with penis, coffin with vagina. Shylock is battered by Tubal's news. The 'Why so' and the "no, no, no!' are as body blows to someone increasingly alone and impotent.

wrecked

81-107 Tubal remains composed, he is outside

Heard in Genoa?

TUBAL Your daughter spent in Genoa, as I heard, one night fourscore ducats.

SHYLOCK Thou stick'st a dagger in me. I shall never see my gold again. Fourscore ducats at a sitting, fourscore ducats?

TUBAL There came divers of Antonio's creditors in my company to Venice that swear he cannot choose but break.°

SHYLOCK I am very glad of it. I'll plague him, I'll torture him. I am glad of it.

TUBAL One of them showed me a ring that he had of your daughter for a monkey.

SHYLOCK Out upon her! Thou torturest me, Tubal. It was my turquoise; I had it of Leah° when I was a bachelor. I would not have given it for a wilderness of monkeys.

TUBAL But Antonio is certainly undone.

SHYLOCK Nay, that's true, that's very true. Go, Tubal, fee me an officer,° bespeak° him a fortnight before. I will have the heart of him if he forfeit, for were he out of Venice I can make° what merchandise I will. Go, Tubal, and meet me at our synagogue.° Go, good Tubal, at our synagogue, Tubal.

Exeunt.

Scene ii Enter BASSANIO, PORTIA, GRATIANO, [NERISSA,] and all their trains.

PORTIA I pray you tarry, pause a day or two
Before you hazard, for in choosing wrong
I lose your company; therefore forbear a while.
There's something tells me—but it is not love—
I would not lose you, and you know yourself
Hate counsels not in such a quality;°
But lest you should not understand me well—

Shylock's maelstrom. He tries to make Shylock's passion bearable by saying Antonio also has ill luck, reinforcing the comparison between the men while broadening the rumour of the ships' disasters. Or does Tubal dole out the information on Jessica by coupling it with Antonio because he's embarrassed to have taken Shylock's money in a fruitless search? Should the second part of the scene be played as a private detective reporting back to his client?

go bankrupt

Shylock's distress is extreme—he repeats, he feeds, he reacts. Shylock's 'I had it off Leah!' is a deep expression of pain—for a moment this cold figure allows his defences to be breached.

When Tubal returns to Antonio, Shylock's energy is now an intense exhaustion. As he plans to get an officer to arrest Antonio the moment the bond is due, he is also determined to take an oath of revenge at his temple. We have seen from Salerio and Solanio that anti-semitism is much wider than Antonio, and so Shylock is here making the same mistake about Antonio as Antonio does about him: each stereotypes the other.

Shylock's wife

hire me a bailiff (to arrest Antonio) contract

will conduct whatever trade I wish

i.e. to swear a solemn oath

Scene ii

1-24 In contrast to the stage directions with 'trains' for Morocco's entrance, and no trains for Aragon's entrance, here Portia brings on 'all their trains'. Is it to impress Bassanio? or show reciprocity? We are back in Belmont, in the casket room.

manner (as I am speaking now)

In the previous casket scenes they were formal and correct, here she is being personal within this public setting. Portia urges him to stay a 'day or two' and then 'some month or two'. Note the con-

And yet a maiden hath no tongue but thought°—
I would detain you here some month or two
Before you venture for me. I could teach you
How to chose right, but then I am forsworn.°
So will I never be; so° may you miss me;
But if you do, you'll make me wish a sin,
That I had been forsworn. Beshrew° your eyes,
They have o'erlooked° me and divided me:
One half of me is yours, the other half yours,
Mine own I would say; but if mine then yours,
And so all yours. O these naughty° times
Puts bars between the owners and their rights;
And so though yours, not yours. Prove it° so,
Let fortune go to hell for it, not I.°
I speak too long, but 'tis to peise° the time,
To eke° it, and to draw it out in length,
To stay you from election.°

BASSANIO Let me choose,
For as I am, I live upon the rack.

PORTIA Upon the rack, Bassanio? Then confess
What treason° there is mingled with your love.

BASSANIO None but that ugly treason of mistrust,°
Which makes me fear th'enjoying of° my love.
There may as well be amity and life
'Tween snow and fire as treason and my love.

PORTIA Ay, but I fear you speak upon the rack
Where men enforced do speak anything.

BASSANIO Promise me life, and I'll confess the truth.

PORTIA Well then, confess and live.

BASSANIO Confess and love
Had been the very sum of my confession.
O happy torment, when my torturer
Doth teach me answers for deliverance!
But let me to my fortune and the caskets.

PORTIA Away then, I am locked in one of them.

i.e. they work simultaneously

will have broken my oath (to obey my father's will)

that...therefore

see II.vi.52

bewitched (by the "evil" eye)

bad

if it prove

i.e. for being forsworn

draw out, extend

increase

(making your) choice

the rack was used to force traitors to confess; Portia speaks playfully

expectancy

fearful about achieving

trasting language: for Morocco and Aragon it was 'choose', for Bassanio it is 'look for me', 'find me', 'come and get me'. As Portia swings between the emotional extremes of 'I could teach you' and 'you may miss me', she shows Bassanio her inner turmoil. There is yearning and frustration in the 'yours' and 'not yours'. She is not mistress of her body, but Bassanio's to win, and her dead father's to give away.

Within everyone's hearing Portia offers to tell him how to choose correctly but pulls back because she knows she must not. Is this further emotional confusion? or is Portia trying to build a rapport, developing a private conversation with Bassanio publicly? Is Bassanio adept, does he listen? or is he impatient to choose?

Portia tacks this way and that. Does the confusion continue? or is it to see whether Bassanio follows her? or to assure the assembled she is not transgressing against the will? or is she scared, and by continuing talk she delays the moment of choice?

24-39 Is Bassanio eager to choose for the same reasons Portia wishes to delay? Note her verbal skills, putting words in his mouth about loving her.

Portia offers to 'teach' Bassanio, and now he asks her to 'teach me answers'. The story of rack and torture shows them playing together: one listens, reacts, builds on the other's story: there is synchronicity between the two. Only when he voluntarily confesses his love, and asks to be taught, does she agree to his choosing.

Or is there also a tension? Does Bassanio insist on choosing immediately because, remembering his promise to Antonio, he is a fortune hunter in a hurry?

40-62 Portia asks everyone to stand away—a

[The curtains are drawn.]

If you do love me, you will find me out.
Nerissa and the rest, stand all aloof.°
Let music sound while he doth make his choice,
Then if he lose he makes a swan-like end,°
Fading in music. That the comparison
May stand more proper,° my eye shall be the stream
And watery deathbed for him. He may win,
And what is music then? Then music is
Even as the flourish° when true subjects bow
To a new-crowned monarch. Such it is
As are those dulcet° sounds in break of day
That creep into the dreaming bridegroom's ear
And summon him to marriage. Now he goes
With no less presence,° but with much more love,
Than young Alcides when he did redeem
The virgin tribute paid by howling Troy
To the sea-monster.° I stand for sacrifice;
The rest aloof are the Dardanian wives,°
With bleared° visages come forth to view
The issue° of th'exploit. Go, Hercules;
Live thou,° I live. With much much more dismay
I view the fight than thou that mak'st the fray.

[Music.] A song, the whilst BASSANIO comments on the caskets to himself.

[One of PORTIA'S musicians.]

Tell me where is fancy° bred,
Or in the heart, or° in the head,
How begot, how nourished?
Reply, reply.

It is engendered in the eyes,
With gazing fed, and fancy dies,
In the cradle° where it lies.
Let us all ring fancy's knell,
I'll begin it: ding, dong, bell.

ALL [Musicians.]

Ding, Dong, bell.

at a distance

the swan was believed to sing only before its death

seem more appropriate

fanfare

sweet

noble bearing

Hercules rescued Hesione from being sacrificed to a sea-monster; however he undertook this for the reward of horses offered by Hesione's father, Laomedon King of Troy, not for love; howling = lamenting

Trojan women

weeping

outcome

if you live

1) love (of a superficial sort, "of the eye" rather than "of the heart") 2) imagination

either…or

1) in the eye 2) in its infancy

request never made for Morocco or Aragon. The caskets are revealed or brought on.

Bassanio goes to read the inscriptions and considers them. Portia tells the story of Hercules rescuing Hesione, not for herself but for her father's horses. Hesione is successfully rescued, but at what cost? Is the sea monster her father's will and his horses Portia? or are the horses her riches and she, like Hesione, is not loved?

By asking the assembled to move to the periphery like the watching Dardanian wives, Portia is staging the scene as if she were Hesione, and in the middle of a play.

63-72 As Bassanio considers, a song is being played. It may not tell him which casket to pick, but how can it not influence him in some way. We already know that Portia and Nerissa are prepared to intervene. The rhyme scheme of the first stanza, bred/head/nourished, rhymes with 'lead'; and the seven beat lines echo the scrolls which carry the authority of Portia's father's voice. There is also the colloctation of fancy/death/coffin, so that when fancy dies to leave true love, it is buried in a coffin, and coffins were frequently lined with lead.

Portia has brought the singer in deliberately. Does the singer make an entrance or emerge from the 'Dardanian wives'? Have the assembled been prompted to sing for Portia's rescue?

BASSANIO So may the outward shows be least themselves;°
The world is still° deceived with ornament.
In law, what plea so tainted and corrupt
But being seasoned with a gracious voice,
Obscures the show of evil. In religion,
What damned error but some sober brow
Will bless it and approve° it with a text,
Hiding the grossness with fair ornament.
There is no vice so simple but assumes
Some mark of virtue on his outward parts.
How many cowards whose hearts are all as false
As stairs of sand, wear yet upon their chins
The beards of Hercules and frowning Mars,
Who inward searched have livers white as milk,°
And these assume but valor's excrement°
To render them redoubted.° Look on beauty
And you shall see 'tis purchased by the weight,°
Which therein works a miracle in nature,
Making them lightest° that wear most of it.
So are those crisped° snaky golden locks
Which make such wanton° gambols° with the wind
Upon supposed fairness,° often known
To be the dowry of a second head,
The skull that bred them in the sepulcher.°
Thus ornament is but the guiled° shore
To a most dangerous sea, the beauteous scarf
Veiling an Indian° beauty; in a word,
The seeming truth which cunning times put on
To entrap the wisest. Therefore then thou gaudy gold,
Hard food for Midas,° I will none of thee;
Nor none of thee, thou pale and common drudge°
[Facing the silver casket]
'Tween man and man.' But thou, thou meager lead,
Which rather threaten'st than dost promise aught,
Thy° paleness moves me more than eloquence,
And here choose I. Joy be the consequence!

PORTIA [Aside.] How all the other passions fleet° to air:
As° doubtful thoughts, and rash-embraced despair,
And shuddering fear, and green-eyed jealousy.
O love, be moderate, allay thy ecstasy,

least like what they really are
continually

73-80 Bassanio's response could come out of contemplating the song or thinking through the clues he has been given or understanding Portia's father. If the last, Bassanio is being aligned with the forces of conservatism; if either of the former, he may be finding Portia on his terms, through their shared understanding.

confirm

81-107 Note that Bassanio picks up the term Hercules, thus sending a small signal to Portia that he has been listening to her. Is this the right moment for Gratiano and Nerissa to withdraw?

Unlike Morocco and Aragon, Bassanio never wrestles with the inscriptions aloud. Throughout he keeps to one point: that appearance and reality are different things, and once begun, he feels sure of his reasoning. In this speech Bassanio is also wresting Portia from the clutches of her father's will; he may be sure but the stakes are high. He dare not put a foot wrong. The audience has more information than the 'Dardanian wives' and this fuller understanding adds to the dramatic tension.

a pale (bloodless) liver was thought to cause cowardice

brave men's beards

feared

alluding to cosmetics

wanton, with a pun on "little value"—"cheap"

curled

1) playful 2) unchaste frisky movements

seeming beauty

endowment to somebody else (in the form of a wig), while the head which grew them lies in the grave

treacherous

East Indian, hence "swarthy" (usually a negative quality to Elizabethans and thus contradictory to "beauty")

Midas whose touch turned everything into gold, including his food

public slave

Thy, to stress the contrast with silver's paleness

fly

such as

108-113 Bassanio chooses lead. Who gives him the key? Have Gratiano and Nerissa re-entered just before he chooses, and does she give him the key? The moment is overwhleming, her agony's resolved here, she is afraid the surge of emotion will kill her.

In measure rain° thy joy, scant° this excess.
I feel too much thy blessing; make it less
For fear I surfeit.°

BASSANIO [Opening the lead casket.] What find I here?
Fair Portia's counterfeit!° What demi-god°
Hath come so near creation? Move these eyes?
Or whether riding on the balls of mine
Seem they in motion? Here are severed lips
Parted with sugar breath, so sweet a bar°
Should sunder such sweet friends.° Here in her hairs
The painter plays the spider, and hath woven
A golden mesh t'entrap the hearts of men
Faster° than gnats in cobwebs. But her eyes,
How could he see to do them? Having made one,
Methinks it should have° power to steal both his
And leave itself unfurnished.° Yet look how far
The substance° of my praise doth wrong this shadow
In underpraising it, so far this shadow°
Doth limp behind the substance.° Here's the scroll,
The continent° and summary of my fortune:

[Reads.]
You that choose not by the view,
Chance as fair° and choose as true.
Since this fortune falls to you,
Be content and seek no new.
If you be well pleased with this
And hold your fortune for your bliss,
Turn you where your lady is
And claim her with a loving kiss.
A gentle scroll. Fair lady, by your leave,
I come by note to give and to receive.°
Like one of two contending in° a prize
That thinks he hath done well in people's eyes,
Hearing applause and universal shout,
Giddy in spirit, still gazing in a doubt
Whether those peals of praise be his° or no,
So, thrice-fair lady, stand I even so,
As doubtful whether what I see be true
Until confirmed, signed, ratified by you.

1) pour 2) rein curtail

sicken with too much

picture i.e. divinely inspired painter

i.e. Portia's breath

separate…lips

more 1) tightly 2) quickly

have had

without its companion

original; i.e. Portia herself

image

imitation

repository

venture as fortunately

Bassanio may kiss Portia here, or later (e.g. line 148, 165 or 174)

for

for him

114-140 As he unlocks it comes Portia's ecstatic aside. What does Bassanio do during her seven lines? Or the rest of the assembled? All can see, though not hear, Portia in her extremis. Does Bassanio watch Portia, but delay opening the casket? Does he open it but is afraid to look?

Is the portrait of Portia a shock, and is Bassanio overwhelmed? Does he look at Portia and compare her with the picture? Does he play the scene with pleasure and humour? or is it Petrarchan conceits, praising Portia's likeness, while making no effort to go to her? or a stunned playing for time? Bassanio has opened the casket, but the dramatic situation is not resolved—the onlookers are not clear whether he has won or lost.

The scroll tells Bassanio he may claim Portia with a loving kiss. The kiss comes after line 140, as in the next lines Bassanio speaks of applause and universal reactions of joy from the assembled. It is most likely to be a reaction to their kissing.

141-174 While savouring and being confused by the applause, he has won Portia, but he also wants to be chosen by her, 'ratifying' him. His speech here has a heightened and rather formal tone, stumbles and sticks on the no, so, so of lines 145-6, as an unsure lover who needs rescuing. It is as if the scene of Hercules and Hesione is replayed, but now rescued and rescuer change places.

Portia suggests she might change her appearance but that she is 'as I am' in need of being

PORTIA You see me, Lord Bassanio, where I stand,
Such as I am. Though for myself alone
I would not be ambitious in my wish
To wish myself much better, yet for you
I would be trebled twenty times myself,
A thousand times more fair, ten thousand times
More rich, that only to stand high in your account
I might in virtues, beauties, livings,° friends,
Exceed account. But the full sum of me
Is sum of something,° which to term in gross°
Is an unlessoned° girl, unschooled, unpractised:
Happy in this, she is not yet so old
But she may learn; happier than this,
She is not bred so dull but she can learn;
Happiest of all, is that her gentle spirit
Commits itself to yours to be directed,
As from her lord, her governor, her king.
Myself, and what is mine, to you and yours
Is now converted.° But° now I was the lord
Of this fair mansion, master of my servants,
Queen o'er myself; and even now, but now,
This house, these servants, and this same myself
Are yours, my lord's. I give them with this ring,
Which when you part from, lose, or give away,
Let it presage° the ruin of your love
And be my vantage to exclaim on you.°

BASSANIO Madam, you have bereft me of all words.
Only my blood speaks to you in my veins,°
And there is such confusion in my powers°
As after some oration fairly spoke
By a beloved prince there doth appear
Among the buzzing, pleased multitude,
Where every something being blent together
Turns to a wild of nothing, save of joy
Expressed and not expressed.° But when this ring
Parts from this finger, then parts life from hence,
O then be bold to say Bassanio's dead.

NERISSA My lord and lady, it is now our time
That have stood by and seen our wishes prosper,

property

at least something 1) in full 2) bluntly

never scolded

made over until

foreshadow

opportunity to accuse you

i.e. in the "noise" of my beating pulse

faculties

individual utterance being mixed together, turns into a hubbub of joy expressed in one general cry rather than through single voices

lessoned, schooled, practised by Bassanio. Her wordplay takes her off any Petrarchan pedestal Bassanio might place her on.

Notice how, after choosing the lead casket, Bassanio follows Portia's rhetorical structures: she moves into rhyming couplets, so does he; she progresses to blank verse and so does he. While she submits herself to his new status of intended husband she is also leading the way. As they woo publicly, getting to know each other, they are also committing to marry.

Does Portia kiss Bassanio after line 161? Portia publicly commits to Bassanio 'This house, these servants, and this same myself'. As the culmination of their exchange Portia gives Bassanio the ring that comes to carry the weight of the whole relationship. Does she kiss him again (line 174)?

175-190 Bassanio seems overwhelmed by emotion and confused by all the applause. Cheering and celebration continues. Bassanio puts the ring on his finger as he searches for words to answer Portia with, yet he doesn't give her a ring. We are celebrating a wedding in the middle of a play; Portia's speech is partly instructing the assembled to treat Bassanio as their new lord.

For the first time (apart from Nerissa's brief interruption), the scene breaks from duologue into a crowd scene. Nerissa formally congratulates Bassanio and Portia on behalf of Belmont, and Gratiano leads the cheering and good wishes on his side.

To cry good joy, good joy, my lord and lady!

GRATIANO My lord Bassanio and my gentle lady,
I wish you all the joy that you can wish,
For I am sure you can wish none from me;°
And when your honors mean to solemnize
The bargain of your faith, I do beseech you
Even at that time I may be married too.

BASSANIO With all my heart, so° thou canst get a wife.

GRATIANO I thank your lordship, you have got me one.
My eyes, my lord, can look as swift as yours:
You saw the mistress, I beheld the maid;
You loved, I loved; for intermission°
No more pertains to me, my lord, than you.
Your fortune stood upon the caskets there,
And so did mine too, as the matter falls;
For wooing here until I sweat again,°
And swearing till my very roof° was dry
With oaths of love, at last—if promise last°—
I got a promise of this fair one here
To have her love, provided that your fortune
Achieved her mistress.

PORTIA Is this true Nerissa?

NERISSA Madam, it is, so you stand pleased withal.

BASSANIO And do you, Gratiano, mean good faith?

GRATIANO Yes, faith, my lord.

BASSANIO Our feast shall be much honored in your marriage.

GRATIANO We'll play° with them the first boy for a thousand ducats.

NERISSA What, and stake down?°

GRATIANO No, we shall ne'er win at that sport and stake down.

Enter LORENZO, JESSICA, and SALERIO a messenger from Venice.

But who comes here? Lorenzo and his infidel.
What, and my old Venetian friend Salerio!

nothing you wish for yourselves can take away from my joy (which is equal to yours); or perhaps "I'm sure you'd never wish the kind of joy a character like me would offer"

191-208 Gratiano too asks to be married. The audience hasn't seen Gratiano with a partner so who does he intend to marry? or is this another Gratiano joke? The dialogue reveals that Gratiano must have been with Bassanio on his first visit, so does Gratiano too have an interest in someone at Belmont?

providing

Just as Bassanio and Portia found each other (if through the caskets), so do Gratiano and Nerissa. Gratiano's request underlines their different status in the play: Gratiano and Nerissa need the permission of their masters.

delay in chosing, loving

sweated again and again

i.e. of my mouth

if Nerissa's promise holds

209-216 With Bassanio's agreement to the double marriage Gratiano, and then Nerissa break the tension of winning wives with crude jokes that relaxes the whole atmosphere.

wager

money put down beforehand; Gratiano's reply puns on the lewd sense "with a limp penis"

217-235 While jesting, Gratiano must move into a position to see Lorenzo, Jessica and Salerio enter.

BASSANIO Lorenzo and Salerio, welcome hither,
If that the youth of my new interest° here
Have power to bid you welcome. By your leave
I bid my very friends and countrymen,
Sweet Portia, welcome.

PORTIA So do I, my lord,
They are entirely welcome.

LORENZO I thank your honor. For my part, my lord,
My purpose was not to have seen you here,
But meeting with Salerio by the way,
He did entreat me past all saying nay
To come with him along.

SALERIO I did, my lord,
And I have reason for it. [Giving a letter.] Signor Antonio
Commends him° to you.

BASSANIO Ere I ope his letter,
I pray you tell me how my good friend doth.

SALERIO Not sick, my lord, unless it be in mind,
Nor well, unless in mind.° His letter there
Will show you his estate.°

[BASSANIO] open[s] the letter [and reads silently.]

GRATIANO Nerissa, cheer yond stranger, bid her welcome.
Your hand, Salerio. What's the news from Venice?
How doth that royal merchant,° good Antonio?
I know he will be glad of our success;
We are the Jasons, we have won the fleece.°

SALERIO I would you had won the fleece° that he hath lost.

PORTIA There are some shrewd° contents in yond same paper
That steals the color from Bassanio's cheek,
Some dear friend dead, else nothing in the world
Could turn so much the constitution
Of any constant man.° What, worse and worse?
With leave, Bassanio, I am half yourself
And I must freely have the half of anything
That this same paper brings you.

the newness of my household authority

His greeting them should indicate surprise. Note that Jessica is still 'his infidel', and that Salerio, who follows the couple onstage, is finally named for the first time.

After the brief respite of jesting in prose, the play returns to verse. With Bassanio's words there are greetings all around. Is Jessica included? Bassanio has never met her. Gratiano does not speak about her until line 237? Jessica's isolation here, like her silences elsewhere, can work to emphasise her otherness from these people.

Portia too welcomes them, but Lorenzo chooses only to address Bassanio. He says Salerio insisted they come along, and then says virtually nothing for the rest of the scene. What were Jessica and Lorenzo doing on the road? and where were they going when their path met up with Salerio's? Is there an overland way to Belmont? Everyone else has come by water.

asks to be remembered

Does Lorenzo speak first, because he is aware of Antonio's predicament. Is this why Salerio asks him to come along? Salerio gives the letter to Bassanio. Salerio's elliptical reply at line 235 leaves 4 empty beats, in which Bassanio opens the letter and begins to read.

his mental fortitude can sustain him

condition

236-241 Gratiano goes back to the celebratory mood, asks Nerissa to welcome Jessica, while he goes to Salerio to find out the latest gossip from Venice.

prince among merchants

see I.i.169-173 and note

i.e. fortune, with a pun on "fleets"

evil, painful

242-266 Bassanio becomes deathly quiet. Is he in trouble here? Despite saying that he had already told her of his relative poverty, what is Portia to think of all the gifts and a large retinue? He must be thinking about saving Antonio, and being less than fulsome with Portia. His difficulty is signalled by hesitations, as 'Gentle lady' and 'yet dear lady', although he manages to tell her the problem.

so much upset the constitution (= state of mind and body) of such a well-balanced man

The audience remembers Bassanio is pledged to Antonio for money, which he intends to repay. That he fails to ask Portia for the money indi-

BASSANIO O sweet Portia,
Here are a few of the unpleasant'st words
That ever blotted paper. Gentle lady,
When I did first impart my love to you,
I freely told you all the wealth I had
Ran in my veins: I was a gentleman,
And then I told you true; and yet, dear lady,
Rating myself at nothing,° you shall see
How much I was a braggart. When I told you
My state° was nothing, I should then have told you
That I was worse than nothing, for indeed
I have engaged° myself to a dear friend,
Engaged my friend to his mere° enemy,
To feed my means. Here is a letter, lady,
The paper as the body of my friend
And every word in it a gaping wound
Issuing life-blood. But is it true, Salerio,
Hath all his ventures failed? What, not one hit°
From Tripolis, from Mexico and England,
From Lisbon, Barbary,° and India,
And not one vessel scape the dreadful touch
Of merchant-marring rocks?

SALERIO Not one, my lord.
Besides, it should appear that if he had
The present° money to discharge the Jew,
He° would not take it. Never did I know
A creature that did bear the shape of man
So keen and greedy to confound° a man.
He plies the Duke at morning and at night,
And doth impeach the freedom of the state°
If they deny him justice. Twenty merchants,
The Duke himself, and the magnificoes°
Of greatest port° have all persuaded° with him,
But none can drive him from the envious° plea
Of forfeiture, of justice, and his bond.

JESSICA When I was with him, I have heard him swear
To Tubal and to Cush, his countrymen,
That he would rather have Antonio's flesh
Than twenty times the value of the sum

cates his embarrassment. He is on the rack of confession.

i.e. at the value of possessing no wealth

personal means

indebted

utter

successful venture

the north African coast

267-290 Is it because Bassanio fails to ask for money that Salerio now goes into such detail about Antonio's fate and Shylock's actions in petitioning for the bond? Does Salerio's speech draw attention to Jessica, as Shylock's daughter? Does she feel compelled to intervene?

Salerio's speech must put Jessica under pressure; she speaks of Shylock in the third person but never names or refers to him as her father. Is she cutting herself off from her past and her culture; they are now 'his countrymen' not hers. It is Jessica who explicitly says that Shylock is after Antonio's flesh.

ready

Shylock

destroy

(threaten to) challenge the state to uphold its rights and freedoms

chief men of Venice

dignity   argued

malicious

That he did owe him; and I know, my lord,
If law, authority, and power deny not,
It will go hard with poor Antonio.

PORTIA Is it your dear friend that is thus in trouble?

BASSANIO The dearest friend to me, the kindest man,
The best-conditioned° and unwearied spirit
In doing courtesies,° and one in whom
The ancient Roman honor more appears
Than any that draws breath in Italy.

PORTIA What sum owes he the Jew?

BASSANIO For me three thousand ducats.

PORTIA What, no more?
Pay him six thousand and deface° the bond.
Double six thousand, and then treble that,
Before a friend of this description
Shall lose a hair through Bassanio's fault.°
First go with me to church and call me wife,
And then away to Venice to your friend,
For never shall you lie by Portia's side
With an unquiet soul. You shall have gold
To pay the petty debt twenty times over.
When it is paid, bring your true friend along.
My maid Nerissa and myself meantime
Will live as maids and widows. Come away,
For you shall hence° upon your wedding day.
Bid your friends welcome, show a merry cheer;°
Since you are dear bought,° I will love you dear.
But let me hear the letter of your friend.

BASSANIO [Reads.] "Sweet Bassanio, my ships have all miscarried, my creditors grow cruel, my estate is very low, my bond to the Jew is forfeit; and since in paying it, it is impossible I should live, all debts are cleared between you and I if I might but see you at my death. Notwithstanding, use your pleasure;° if your love do not persuade you to come, let not my letter."

PORTIA O love, dispatch all business and be gone.

best-natured

good deeds, not just "polite gestures"

cancel

default, as well as the usual sense

go from here

aspect

gained 1) lovingly 2) at a high price

follow your own inclinations

291-301 Bassanio stays silent throughout, and only responds when Portia asks about 'your dear friend'. He picks up her phrase and intensifies it, his language unbottles for the first time. Portia must sense this outpouring of superlatives for someone else. Presumably she calls Shylock the 'Jew' because he has not been named in her presence. It carries on the distancing started by Jessica, allowing stereotypes to flower.

When Bassanio finally tells her how much he owes, she makes light of it and says she will 'double' and 'treble' and pay 'twenty times' the debt. Is the undercurrent irony an echo with her earlier speech in which she gives herself 'trebled twenty times'? Despite Antonio having been named three times in this scene she impersonalises him to 'a friend' and 'your friend'.

302-312 Even as Bassanio says he must leave immediately, she reminds him they are to be married. Does he forget? Is there a rival for her affection? Lines 305-6 can be played as Portia thinking through the situation, improvising. She continues to distance Antonio by calling him 'your true friend' and uses the phrase 'maids and widows' of herself and Nerissa, as if experiencing a bereavement to the person she thought she had fallen in love with. Does she now need to fall in love with another person, one more complex, with a messy history?

Bassanio is transfixed, nothing has changed, and so she has to pursue her argument, and moves to the ambivalent 'Since you are dear bought, I will love you dear' (l.312). This has a strong undercurrent of recognition that Bassanio wants her for the money. It makes her analogous with Antonio: both of them have bought Bassanio.

313-325 Bassanio continues to be silent, so Portia asks to hear the letter, which will not only tell her its contents and something about Antonio's and Bassanio's relationship, even in the way he reads it.

Her tone changes. Note the supportive (if monetary) urgency in Portia's 'dispatch all business'. At these words Bassanio is finally able to speak.

BASSANIO Since I have your good leave to go away,
I will make haste; but till I come again,
No bed shall e'er be guilty of my stay
Nor rest be interposer twixt us twain. Exeunt.

Scene iii Enter [SHYLOCK] the JEW, and SOLANIO, and ANTONIO, and the JAILER.

SHYLOCK Jailer, look to him. Tell not me of mercy.
This is the fool that lent out money gratis.
Jailer, look to him.

ANTONIO Hear me yet, good Shylock.

SHYLOCK I'll have my bond, speak not against my bond.
I have sworn an oath that I will have my bond.
Thou calledst me dog before thou hadst a cause,
But since I am a dog, beware my fangs.
The Duke shall grant me justice. I do wonder,
Thou naughty° jailer, that thou art so fond°
To come abroad° with him at his request.

ANTONIO I pray thee hear me speak.

SHYLOCK I'll have my bond. I will not hear thee speak.
I'll have my bond, and therefore speak no more.
I'll not be made a soft and dull-eyed° fool,
To shake the head, relent, and sigh, and yield
To Christian intercessors. Follow not.
I'll have no speaking, I will have my bond.

Exit [SHYLOCK the] JEW.

SOLANIO It is the most impenetrable cur
That ever kept° with men.

ANTONIO Let him alone,
I'll follow him no more with bootless° prayers.
He seeks my life, his reason well I know:
I oft delivered from his forfeitures°

'Business' refers to their getting married. Money and commerce go hand in hand with their relationship.

Scene iii

1-17 Antonio is trying to meet up with Shylock in the street under prison guard. Does Shylock meet him coming from the opposite direction, or is he getting away? From Shylock's opening remark—a reply to something that has just been said?—the jailer is standing away from Antonio and Solanio. Shylock's comment 'tell me not of mercy' will play a crucial part later on; here he publicly makes fun of Antonio. Getting his own back? His jokes are about money rather than race.

For the first time in the play Antonio is not in control, he has to interrupt Shylock with 'Hear me yet'. Shylock overrides his plea and reiterates the insults that Antonio cast at him, reminding the audience the real problem here is the abuse he has received. In Peter Zadek's production for the Berliner Ensemble, Shylock "goes into a long, mocking routine that involves confusing Antonio's body odour with dog muck on his own shoe." (The Times, 1995). Shylock is beginning to feel a sense of power—he implicitly threatens by twice asking Antonio to be taken back to jail. He can afford not to listen.

wicked foolish

outside

easily deceived

Line eleven has four silent beats. Does Shylock exit in these? Antonio fights for his attention, Shylock's answer is 'Follow not'. Antonio's 'Let him alone' suggests Solanio is going after Shylock, while Antonio accepts that Shylock's position is unchangeable.

dwelt

18-36 Solanio tries to give Antonio hope. Antonio is clear the course of law cannot be denied, or justice will be discredited. Is Solanio in this scene because he is in love with Antonio? How does he react when urged to leave? Does he leave separately? Antonio's final hope is to see Bassanio before he dies.

fruitless

penalties (for default in payment)

Many that have at times made moan to me,
Therefore he hates me.

SOLANIO I am sure the Duke
Will never grant this forfeiture to hold.

ANTONIO The Duke cannot deny the course of law,
For the commodity° that strangers° have
With us in Venice, if it be denied,
Will much impeach° the justice of the state,
Since that the trade and profit of the city
Consisteth of all nations. Therefore go.
These griefs and losses have so bated° me
That I shall hardly spare a pound of flesh
Tomorrow to my bloody creditor.
Well, jailer, on. Pray God Bassanio come
To see me pay his debt, and then I care not. Exeunt.

Scene iv Enter PORTIA, NERISSA, LORENZO, JESSICA, and [BALTHAZAR] a man of PORTIA'S.

LORENZO Madam, although I speak it in your presence,
You have a noble and a true conceit°
Of god-like amity°, which appears most strongly
In bearing thus the absence of your lord.
But if you knew to whom you show this honor,
How true a gentleman you send relief,
How dear a lover° of my lord your husband,
I know you would be prouder of the work
Than customary bounty can enforce you.°

PORTIA I never did repent for doing good,
Nor shall not now; for in companions
That do converse and waste° the time together,
Whose souls do bear an equal yoke of love,
There must be needs° a like proportion
Of lineaments, of manners, and of spirit,
Which makes me think that this Antonio,

commercial liberties for-
eigners (including Jews)

call into question

1) reduced 2) depressed

Scene iv

understanding

friendship

friend

ordinary acts of kindness
allow you to feel

spend

of necessity

1-21 Portia unexpectedly calls Lorenzo, Jessica, Nerissa and Stephano together. Do Lorenzo and Jessica enter with her, but Nerissa and Stephano come from elsewhere? We do not know how long Gratiano and Bassanio have been gone. Lorenzo's rhetoric is formal: is he, a stranger, trying to create a friendship with Portia and reassure her about Bassanio? Why are they still here? They have no role in the household, and their friend Bassanio has left. Have they spent all of Jessica's money with nowhere to go?

In this speech, ostensibly about Bassanio, she mentions Antonio by name for the first time. Portia reasons that Antonio must be like Bassanio. Is she wondering whether there is room for her in such a relationship; or does she feel strongly for Antonio since she has just been freed from bondage that he is in? Portia keeps the veneer of formality going, answering Lorenzo in her final lines. As Portia speaks line 21, we should be aware of Jessica's presence, whose father is being spoken about.

Being the bosom lover of my lord,
Must needs be like my lord. If it be so,
How little is the cost I have bestowed
In purchasing the semblance° of my soul
From out the state of hellish cruelty.
This comes too near the praising of myself,
Therefore no more of it. Hear other things:
Lorenzo, I commit into your hands
The husbandry and manage° of my house
Until my lord's return. For mine own part
I have toward heaven breathed a secret vow
To live in prayer and contemplation,
Only attended by Nerissa here
Until her husband and my lord's return.
There is a monastery two miles off,
And there we will abide. I do desire you
Not to deny this imposition,°
The which my love and some necessity
Now lays upon you.

LORENZO Madam, with all my heart,
I shall obey you in all fair commands.

PORTIA My people° do already know my mind
And will acknowledge you and Jessica
In place of Lord Bassanio and myself.
So fare you well till we shall meet again.

LORENZO Fair thoughts and happy hours attend on you.

JESSICA I wish your ladyship all heart's content.

PORTIA I thank you for your wish, and am well pleased
To wish it back on you. Fare you well Jessica.
Exeunt [LORENZO and JESSICA.]
Now, Balthazar,
As I have ever found thee honest true,
So let me find thee still: take this same letter
And use thou all th'endeavor of a man
In speed to Padua; see thou render this
Into my cousin's hands, Doctor Bellario,
And look what notes and garments he doth give thee;
Bring them, I pray thee, with imagined speed°

likeness; i.e. Antonio is Bassanio's second self and thus also a "soul-mate" of Portia's

ordering and management

refuse this task

household

all imaginable speed

22-44 Portia changes tone and responds to Lorenzo within the parameters of the information he puts forward, as if carefully hiding any traces of her plan. She puts Lorenzo in charge of Belmont while she and Nerissa go live in prayer until their husband's return. Lorenzo is eager to take up the request.

Lorenzo and Jessica are the last to know that Portia is leaving, yet she has already asked her household to obey them. Portia explicitly makes a parallel between Jessica and herself, underlining Jessica's silence. We have not seen Lorenzo speak a word to her since they ran away. Portia gives her a voice that Lorenzo seems insensitive to.

Does this focus also critique the way Bassanio and Gratiano show warmth to their world of male friends as they go off to help Antonio? Does this also apply to Lorenzo?

Portia absorbs Lorenzo's reply but responds to Jessica's, which is more personal and recognises her unease. Lorenzo and Jessica exit, and just as they are about to leave, Jessica runs back to Portia. Portia is pleased but limits the conversation because she has other plans.

45-56 Keeping one story alive for her household and Jessica and Lorenzo, the audience with Nerissa learns there is another plan afoot. Portia, having submitted to her father's will, now being won and released, is taking control of her life and going into the outside world.

Portia four times addresses Balthazar as 'thee', underlining the urgency of her request. This part of Portia's plan makes no naturalistic sense: How, for example, does she expect to insinuate herself into the courtroom?

Unto the traject,° to the common° ferry
Which trades to Venice. Waste no time in words
But get thee gone; I shall be there before thee.

BALTHAZAR Madam, I go with all convenient° speed. [Exit.]

PORTIA Come on, Nerissa, I have work in hand
That you yet know not of. We'll see our husbands
Before they think of us.

NERISSA Shall they see us?

PORTIA They shall, Nerissa, but in such a habit°
That they shall think we are accomplished°
With that we lack.° I'll hold thee any wager
When we are both accoutred° like young men
I'll prove the prettier° fellow of the two,
And wear my dagger with the braver grace,
And speak between the change of man and boy
With a reed voice,° and turn two mincing steps
Into a manly stride, and speak of frays
Like a fine bragging youth, and tell quaint° lies
How honorable ladies sought my love,
Which I denying, they fell sick and died —
I could not do withal!° Then I'll repent
And wish for all° that, that I had not killed them;
And twenty of these puny lies I'll tell,
That men shall swear I have discontinued school
Above a twelvemonth.° I have within my mind
A thousand raw tricks of these bragging jacks°
Which I will practise.

NERISSA Why, shall we turn to° men?

PORTIA Fie, what a question's that,
If thou wert near a lewd interpreter.
But come, I'll tell thee all my whole device
When I am in my coach, which stays for us
At the park gate; and therefore haste away,
For we must measure twenty miles today. Exeunt.

ferry public

possible

dress; i.e. disguise

equipped

i.e. male features

apparelled

finer, more manly

i.e. as though my voice were breaking

clever

help it

in spite of

for at least a year

fellows

turn into (with a pun on "sexually pursue")

57-85 When Portia turns to Nerissa, it becomes clear that this plan has nothing to do with a monastery.

Line 59 has an edge to it that belies the women's interest in their husbands, prompting them into another change of mood: one of earthiness, sexuality, irreverance and banter. The women allow themselves to joke and indulge in the bawdy wordplay of 1.2. Here they go further as the audience watches them making a transition into men. As Portia speaks, so she enacts the high voice, mincing steps of a woman, the bragging front of a man. Not necessarily moment by moment, but in high spirits and playing with the detail of her knowledge. The implication is that gender is socially constituted.

Is the scene's function partly to make the audience laugh so that when we come to the trial we already accept them as men? Nerissa's question about getting dressed up like men emphasises the strangeness of the action, and indicates a hesitation if not reluctance that deepens the nervous energy of the comedy.

Time reasserts itself, the tone changes: speed is of the essence. Line 82 shows her having to cajole Nerissa. Is Nerissa annoyed at not having been consulted? or is she frightened? Does she still feel in charge? or fear that as a servant she has too much to lose?

Scene v Enter [LAUNCELOT the] clown and JESSICA.

LAUNCELOT Yes truly, for look you, the sins of the father are to be laid upon the children; therefore, I promise you, I fear° you. I was always plain with you, and so now I speak my agitation° of the matter; therefore be o'good cheer, for truly I think you are damned. There is but one hope in it that can do you any good, and that is but a kind of bastard hope neither.°

JESSICA And what hope is that, I pray thee?

LAUNCELOT Marry, you may partly hope that your father got° you not, that you are not the Jew's daughter.

JESSICA That were a kind of bastard hope indeed; so the sins of my mother should be visited upon me.

LAUNCELOT Truly then I fear you are damned both by father and mother; thus when I shun Scylla your father, I fall into Charbydis° your mother. Well, you are gone both ways.

JESSICA I shall be saved by my husband.° He hath made me a Christian.

LAUNCELOT Truly, the more to blame he. We were Christians enough before, e'en as many as could well live one by another.° This making of Christians will raise the price of hogs; if we grow all to be pork-eaters, we shall not shortly have a rasher° on the coals for money.

Enter LORENZO.

JESSICA I'll tell my husband, Launcelot, what you say. Here he comes.

LORENZO I shall grow jealous of you shortly, Launcelot, if you thus get my wife into corners.

JESSICA Nay, you need not fear us, Lorenzo, Launcelot and I are

Scene v

fear for

blunder for "cogitation" = consideration

anyway

begot

1-22 Until Launcelot's exit, the scene is in prose. Is its purpose to give Portia and Nerissa time to get to Venice? When we last saw Launcelot and Jessica he was the go-between and she single. Now he is the fool and Jessica married.

Her change in status, as a married woman and a Christian, makes Jessica fair game for his foolery. He hones in, not on marriage but her converted state. He 'jokes' that she might hope to be a bastard, and therefore not the daughter of a Jew.

Jessica's reply is surprisingly confident, though she urges him to further foolery. Jessica calls Lorenzo 'my husband'. It is the first explicit evidence we have of their marriage. For the first time since leaving Shylock's house, Jessica is more than a peripheral figure. She is still alone, and her being forthcoming with Launcelot furthers this impression.

two hazards, respectively a monster and a whirlpool, Ulysses had to sail through in The Odyssey, 12.18

I Corinthians 7:14

1) side by side 2) off of one another

i.e. of bacon

23-60 Lorenzo seems to recognise this, as he part jests about his jealousy. He is aware of Launcelot's reputation as sexual predator; and Jessica plays on this by saying she and Launcelot 'are out'. Is Jessica angry? or just trying to keep the joking going? Yet she repeats the conversation for Lorenzo.

out.° He tells me flatly there's no mercy for me in heaven because I am a Jew's daughter, and he says you are no good member of the commonwealth,° for in converting Jews to Christians, you raise the price of pork.

LORENZO [To LAUNCELOT.] I shall answer that better to the commonwealth than you can the getting up of the Negro's belly;° the Moor is with child by you, Launcelot.

LAUNCELOT It is much that the Moor should be more° than reason,° but if she be less than an honest woman, she is indeed more than I took her for.

LORENZO How every fool can play upon the word. I think the best grace° of wit will shortly turn into silence, and discourse grow commendable in none only but parrots. Go in, sirrah, bid them prepare for dinner.

LAUNCELOT That is done, sir, they have all stomachs.°

LORENZO Goodly Lord, what a wit-snapper are you! Then bid them prepare dinner.

LAUNCELOT That is done too, sir, only "cover"° is the word.

LORENZO Will you cover then, sir?

LAUNCELOT Not so, sir, neither. I know my duty.

LORENZO Yet more quarrelling with occasion.° Wilt thou show the whole wealth of thy wit in an instant? I pray thee understand a plain man in his plain meaning: go to thy fellows, bid them cover the table, serve in the meat,° and we will come in to dinner.

LAUNCELOT For the table,° sir, it shall be served in; for the meat, sir, it shall be covered;° for your coming in to dinner, sir, why let it be as humors and conceits° shall govern.

Exit [LAUNCELOT the] CLOWN.

LORENZO O dear discretion,° how his words are suited.°
The fool hath planted in his memory
An army of good words, and I do know
A many fools that stand in better place,°
Garnished° like him, that for a tricksy° word

at odds

society

i.e. making her pregnant. This is all we hear about this servant

Launcelot puns on the similar pronunciations

greater than what is reasonable

highest quality

appetites

lay the table; but Launcelot then changes the sense (l.54) to mean "wear one's hat"

quibbling on the slightest pretext

food

the food

i.e. kept (hot) in covered dishes

whims and opinions

common sense made to fit the occasion

1) higher, or 2) other social positions

1) dressed (see II.vi.44 and note) 2) supplied with words rascally

A production can play this repetition in different ways: to present Jessica as confident, wounded, manipulative, or angry. Does it show their having a trusting relationship? or do they, as yet, have little to say? Jessica once more becomes quiet.

Lorenzo has been in search of Launcelot, who has impregnated one of Portia's servants. Significantly in this play about ethnicity, the servant is a 'Moor', but we hear nothing else about her. Launcelot is not called to account for his actions, but engages in wordplay instead.

Throughout the exchanges between Lorenzo and Launcelot that follow, Lorenzo tries to act the head of the household, at first dismissing Launcelot as a servant, trying to beat him at wordplay while emphasising his displeasure. Launcelot's response is to take greater liberties.

He is Bassanio's fool, and Bassanio is the lord of the house. Unlike Jessica, Lorenzo tries to deal with criticism by squashing it. In a sense the scene has been a moral lesson in how to deal with criticism which is to the point. If you try to deny it or order it away, it simply gets stronger. If you play back at it on its terms it may self-destruct. Lorenzo has simply not had the experience in this field that Jessica has.

Defy the matter.° How cheer'st thou,° Jessica?
And now, good sweet, say thy opinion:
How dost thou like the Lord Bassanio's wife?

JESSICA Past all expressing. It is very meet°
The Lord Bassanio live an upright life,
For having such a blessing in his lady
He finds the joys of heaven here on earth,
And if on earth he do not merit it,°
In reason° he should never come to heaven.
Why, if two gods should play some heavenly match
And on the wager lay° two earthly women,
And Portia one, there must be something else
Pawned° with the other, for the poor rude world
Hath not her fellow.

LORENZO Even such a husband
Hast thou of me, as she is for a wife.

JESSICA Nay, but ask my opinion too of that!

LORENZO I will anon, first let us go to dinner.

JESSICA Nay, let me praise you while I have a stomach.°

LORENZO No, pray thee, let it serve for table-talk,
Then howsome'er° thou speak'st, 'mong other things
I shall digest° it.

JESSICA Well, I'll set you forth.° *Exeunt.*

plainly intended sense

is it with you?

fitting

i.e. live the virtuous life that being blessed with Portia obliges him to lead

it follows

stake

wagered in addition; i.e. to make up Portia's full value

1) appetite 2) inclination

however

endure, "stomach," as well as the usual sense

1) dish you up 2) praise you

61-82 After Launcelot's departure, Lorenzo turns to her in his need to explain him away. Is Lorenzo moderating his reaction to Launcelot now that he is alone with Jessica? Or is he using language to cover the silence between them? is the affectionate 'cheer'st' the occasion for a kiss? It seems to resolve something, for Lorenzo goes on to something new. Nonetheless there is an awkwardness in the formality of Lorenzo's question at lines 62-63, and Jessica answers in language so heightened that it gives an odd indication of desire to be someone else.

Jessica praises Portia out of her earshot. Does this imply Jessica's blessing in the coming courtroom confrontation with Shylock?

Jessica's seriousness is deflated somewhat by Lorenzo who sets her up to praise him in the terms she has used for Portia. Jessica immediately picks up the lighter tone, and Lorenzo delays his response because he knows what he is inviting.

The audience is watching a parallel scene of wordplay which is there to bolster the person feeling vulnerable. It underlines the way that Launcelot has licence to make fun, but Jessica, the obedient wife, must make the jokes serve her husband's purpose.

The scene as a whole is a demonstration of the interaction of status and humour. In the first encounter Jessica beats down Launcelot, or they are evenly matched; in the second, Launcelot wins outright; and in the third, Jessica gives way, which the audience can see as a self-conscious gesture of obedience. Class, gender and race are displayed here as inextricably intertwined.

ACT IV

Scene i Enter the DUKE, the MAGNIFICOES,° ANTONIO, BASSANIO, [SALERIO,] and GRATIANO.

DUKE What, is Antonio here?

ANTONIO Ready, so please your grace.

DUKE I am sorry for thee. Thou art come to answer°
A stony adversary, an inhuman wretch,
Uncapable of pity, void and empty
From any dram° of mercy.

ANTONIO I have heard
Your grace hath ta'en great pains to qualify°
His rigorous course; but since he stands obdurate,
And that no lawful means can carry me
Out of his envy's° reach, I do oppose
My patience to his fury, and am armed
To suffer with a quietness of spirit
The very tyranny and rage of his.

DUKE Go one, and call the Jew into the court.

SALERIO He is ready at the door; he comes, my lord.

Enter SHYLOCK.

DUKE Make room, and let him stand before our° face.
Shylock, the world thinks, and I think so too,
That thou but lead'st this fashion° of thy malice
To the last hour of act, and then 'tis thought
Thou'lt show thy mercy and remorse° more strange°
Than is thy strange° apparent cruelty;
And where thou now exacts the penalty,
Which is a pound of this poor merchant's flesh,

see III.ii.279 and note

ACT IV. Scene i

defend yourself against

"drop"

mitigate

malice's

1-15 The scene can adequately begin with the named characters, plus a couple of Magnificoes. But 'What, is Antonio here?' may make more sense if the Duke searches him out in a crowded courtroom.

The line also calls the court to order, and Antonio's reply 'Ready' can mean both 'I am here' and 'I am prepared'. The Duke offers Antonio his sympathy, although the law must take its course. Antonio is concerned to show himself willing to submit to the law. This exchange firmly puts the motivation for what follows into Shylock's hands.

the royal plural denoting princely authority; the Duke switches in the next line to "I" to make a personal appeal

are only making this show

pity strikingly

unheard-of

16-34 Shylock's absence creates anticipation. He gets his own entrance. Note that Shylock enters alone while Antonio is surrounded by friends: the staging can choose to underline this difference throughout the scene. The Duke's 'make room' suggests Shylock is being impeded. The Duke brings the court to order a second time, creating pace.

Having called him 'Jew' before he enters, the Duke now calls Shylock by name and immedi-

Thou wilt not only loose° the forfeiture,
But, touched with human gentleness and love,
Forgive a moiety° of the principal,
Glancing an eye of pity on his losses
That have of late so huddled on his back,
Enough to press a royal merchant° down
And pluck commiseration of° his state
From brassy° bosoms and rough hearts of flints,
From stubborn Turks and Tartars° never trained
To offices° of tender courtesy.°
We all expect° a gentle answer, Jew.

SHYLOCK I have possessed° your grace of what I purpose,
And by our holy Sabbath have I sworn
To have the due and forfeit of my bond;
If you deny it, let the danger° light
Upon your charter and your city's freedom.°
You'll ask me why I rather choose to have
A weight of carrion flesh than to receive
Three thousand ducats. I'll not answer that,
But say it is my humor.° Is it answered?
What if my house be troubled with a rat
And I be pleased to give ten thousand ducats
To have it baned?° What, are you answered yet?
Some men there are love not a gaping pig,°
Some that are mad if they behold a cat,
And others when the bagpipe sings i'th'nose
Cannot contain their urine; for affection,
Mistress of passion,° sways it to the mood
Of what it likes or loathes. Now for your answer:
As there is no firm reason to be rendered
Why he° cannot abide a gaping pig,
Why he a harmless° necessary cat,
Why he a woollen bagpipe but of force°
Must yield to such inevitable shame
As to offend himself° being offended,
So can I give no reason, nor I will not,
More than a lodged° hate and a certain° loathing
I bear Antonio, that I follow thus
A losing° suit against him. Are you answered?

ately suggests a strategy for him to pull back from enforcing the bond. In stark contrast to the way he speaks about Shylock in his absence, the Duke now tries to persuade Shylock to turn apparent cruelty into actual mercy.

The exchange allows both Duke and Shylock to publicly state their positions in court, and serves as a formal introduction to the proceedings. The Duke is using the authority of his office to persuade, in effect inviting Shylock to be part of Christian Venice when he sets 'gentle'/gentile off next to 'Jew'. The way his speech twice addresses Shylock, and in quite different ways, helps develop the character away from potential stereotype.

35-62 Standing before him all the while Shylock replies that he has taken a holy oath, which goes directly to the weakness of the state's argument. He then pre-empts the Duke by anticipating his next question.

He is so certain of his case that he plays with the Duke. To say that his desire for the pound of 'dead flesh' is but 'my humour' both answers capriciously and provokes. Dustin Hoffman's Shylock "carries a sense of ironic vindictivness with him into the trial scene. Hoffman flashed smiles at the Venetian judges as he insists on the letter of his bond—see, I'm acting the heartless Jew, he seems to be saying" (The Spectator, 1989).

The dynamics of the scene, and Shylock's prompt to the Duke and the others 'are you answer'd yet' indicate they are, dumbfounded by his reply and the directness of feeling.

Shylock's 'now for your answer' sustains the idea of silence, but can also be a way of stopping the Duke from interrupting. Shylock moves from offering a reason, that his 'humour' or character demands the bond, to admitting that he can give no reason and will not. The actor could play this as someone who realises there is no real basis for claiming the bond, despite all his railing against Antonio for depriving him of money. Or he may want to keep silent about this aspect of his character. The latter reinforces the feeling of victimisation by the society around him. Shylock finishes with a fifth 'are you answered?'.

remit

portion

prince among merchants

with

hard like brass; i.e. unfeeling

stubborn because resisting belief in Christianity

performing services

tender courtesy of a kind and civilized nature

await, as well as "look forward to as essential"

informed

harm

see III.ii.277-8

characteristic temperament, and/or whim

poisoned

roasted pig (served) with its mouth open

affection = instinctive disposition (or "humor" l.43), passion = the range of emotional responses; thus, "instinct controls or determines our emotional reaction in any given situation"

one person…another…yet another

naturally harmless

involuntarily

i.e. l.50 "Cannot contain their urine"

deep-seated fixed

unprofitable

BASSANIO This is no answer, thou unfeeling man,
To excuse the current° of thy cruelty.

SHYLOCK I am not bound to please thee with my answers.

BASSANIO Do all men kill the things they do not love?

SHYLOCK Hates any man the thing he would not kill?

BASSANIO Every offence is not a hate at first.

SHYLOCK What, wouldst thou have a serpent sting thee twice?

ANTONIO I pray you think you question° with the Jew.
You may as well go stand upon the beach
And bid the main flood bate his° usual height;
You may as well use question° with the wolf
Why he hath made the ewe bleat for the lamb;
You may as well forbid the mountain pines
To wag° their high tops and to make no noise
When they are fretten° with the gusts of heaven;
You may as well do anything most hard
As seek to soften that—than which what's harder?—
His Jewish heart. Therefore I do beseech you
Make no more offers, use no farther means,
But with all brief and plain conveniency°
Let me have judgement, and the Jew his will.

BASSANIO For thy three thousand ducats here is six.

SHYLOCK If every ducat in six thousand ducats
Were in six parts, and every part a ducat,
I would not draw° them, I would have my bond.

DUKE How shalt thou hope for mercy rendering none?

SHYLOCK What judgement shall I dread doing no wrong?
You have among you many a purchased slave,
Which like your asses and your dogs and mules
You use in abject and in slavish parts°
Because you bought them. Shall I say to you,
"Let them be free, marry them to your heirs.
Why sweat they under burdens? Let their beds
Be made as soft as yours, and let their palates
Be seasoned with such viands."° You will answer

course

63-87 Seeing Shylock's implacability at first hand, Bassanio intervenes. He argues with Shylock on the basis of 'humours', makes sure to call him 'unfeeling man' not 'Jew'. Shylock's reply has a sarcastic edge, for he is not bound to Bassanio, and at the same time it asserts his power to ignore Bassanio and speak to the court. Bassanio then engages, courteously, in a word fight with Shylock and he responds by sending each argument back. Shylock continues to stand in front of the Duke.

Antonio and the Duke have been through this debate with Shylock. Antonio calms Bassanio down, absolving him from any personal responsibility in his impending death. Note Antonio repeats 'You may as well' four times in the build up to 'his Jewish heart'. Is he residually still trying to shame Shylock into changing his mind?

remember you are arguing

high tide abate its

dispute

Antonio implores Bassanio to desist, as Bassanio keeps trying to argue with Shylock. Although Antonio manages to turn the attention back to the court, Bassanio offers Shylock money, which is rejected. This interaction focuses not only on the two men, but also on Shylock's reaction. Does Antonio enjoy or uncomfortably recognise the growing sense of loss? Is he impatient for the case to get underway?

shake, without the modern connotation of playfulness

fretted; i.e. ruffled

propriety

take

88-110 The Duke again takes control of the proceedings, challenging Shylock to explain himself. Once more Shylock answers in exactly balanced terms: he is only behaving as Venetian society behaves. If mercy is to be an indicator of humanity, why does Venice keep slaves? He goes on at length about Venetian treatment of slaves, yet refrains from a moral condemnation. In asking for judgment, Shylock is showing that the laws of Venice operate without morality.

capacities

The Duke now introduces something new and unexpected to the court, that Bellario is coming. While Antonio anticipates this as his last day alive,

food such as yours

"The slaves are ours." So do I answer you.
The pound of flesh which I demand of him
Is dearly bought, 'tis mine and I will have it.
If you deny me, fie upon your law,
There is no force in the decrees of Venice.
I stand for judgement. Answer: shall I have it?

DUKE Upon my power I may dismiss this court,
Unless Bellario, a learned doctor°
Whom I have sent for to determine this,
Come here today.

SALERIO My lord, here stays without°
A messenger with letters from the doctor,
New come from Padua.

DUKE Bring us the letters. Call the messenger.
[Exit SALERIO.]

BASSANIO Good cheer, Antonio. What, man, courage yet!
The Jew shall have my flesh, blood, bones and all,
Ere thou shalt lose for me one drop of blood.

ANTONIO I am a tainted wether° of the flock,
Meetest° for death. The weakest kind of fruit
Drops earliest to the ground, and so let me.
You cannot better be employed, Bassanio,
Than to live still and write mine epitaph.

Enter [SALERIO with] NERISSA [disguised as a judge's clerk.]

DUKE Came you from Padua, from Bellario?

NERISSA From both, my lord. [Presenting a letter.] Bellario greets your grace.

[SHYLOCK whets his knife on his shoe.]

BASSANIO Why dost thou whet thy knife so earnestly?

SHYLOCK To cut the forfeiture from that bankrupt there.

GRATIANO Not on thy sole but on thy soul, harsh Jew,
Thou mak'st thy knife keen; but no metal can —
No, not the hangman's° axe—bear half the keenness

and Shylock thinks it is his day in court, the Duke, unbeknown to either party, asks for an outside prosecutor. Has the scene so far, therefore, been a tactic of delay by the Duke? Is that why he allows Bassanio to interrupt? Theatrically it works to dramatise the reports of the Duke's compassion, to show Shylock's intransigence, Antonio's desperation, as well as the involvement of Bassanio.

i.e. doctor of law, as elsewhere in this scene

Salerio is able to say that a messenger has arrived from Bellario. How does he know? Has he been told? or should he leave the room earlier, say line 90, which might also prompt the Duke's line about Bellario?

waits outside

The Duke calls for the messenger. There is anticipation and delay: the audience's anticipation of seeing Nerissa as a man, the silence of the Duke, the hubbub in the court, Bassanio's and Antonio's conversation. Shylock now moves to the side, to a stool or a table—the trial is beginning in earnest. In Dustin Hoffman's portrayal "Expert at anticipating slights, this Jew pre-empts the possibility of being refused a seat in the trial scene by placing himself down on the suitcase in which he has carried his scales' (The Independent, 1989).

sickly (castrated) ram

fittest

111-120 When Nerissa enters, she has two lines to travel to the Duke and hand him a letter. This gives the audience its first chance to see her in men's clothes, and test whether Bassanio or Gratiano recognises her. Having rooted her entrance in the action of handing over the letter, the scene now switches attention back to Shylock.

121-148 Instead of focusing on Nerissa and the Duke, Bassanio and Gratiano and Antonio watch Shylock sharpening his knife on the soles of his leather shoes. Bassanio is reduced to horrified silence.

executioner's

While the Duke reads the letter, Gratiano tries to provoke Shylock. But his lack of subtlety, his passion gives Shylock the measure of Gratiano. To

Of thy sharp envy.° Can no prayers pierce thee?

SHYLOCK No, none that thou hast wit enough to make.

GRATIANO O be thou damned, inexecrable° dog,
And for thy life let justice be accused!°
Thou almost mak'st me waver in my faith°
To hold opinion with Pythagoras,°
That souls of animals infuse themselves
Into the trunks of men. Thy currish spirit
Governed° a wolf who hanged for human slaughter;°
Even from the gallows did his fell° soul fleet,°
And, whilst thou lay'st in thy unhallowed dam,°
Infused itself in thee, for thy desires
Are wolfish, bloody, starved, and ravenous.

SHYLOCK Till thou canst rail the seal from off my bond,
Thou but offend'st thy lungs to speak so loud.
Repair thy wit, good youth, or it will fall
To cureless ruin. I stand here for law.

DUKE This letter from Bellario doth commend
A young and learned doctor to our° court.
Where is he?

NERISSA He attendeth here hard by°
To know your answer whether you'll admit him.

DUKE With all my heart. Some three or four of you
Go give him courteous conduct to this place.

[Exeunt several of the court.]

Meantime the court shall hear Bellario's letter:

[Reads.]

"Your grace shall understand that at the receipt of your letter I am very sick, but in the instant that your messenger came, in loving visitation° was with me a young doctor of Rome: his name is Balthazar. I acquainted him with the cause in controversy between the Jew and Antonio the merchant. We turned o'er many books together. He is furnished with my opinion which, bettered with his own learning—the greatness whereof I cannot enough commend—comes with him at my importunity to fill up° your grace's request in my stead. I

malice

Gratiano's verbiage, Shylock remains provocatively silent, or answers curtly.

Gratiano develops an elaboration of Shylock as a dog, but as he moves from being impassioned to being caught up in his own imagery. Shylock continues sharpening his knife, his voice may well be lazy and quiet to Gratiano's loudness. Shylock is so confident about his case in law that, uncharacteristically, he allows himself humour. 'I stand here for law' draws attention to his being seated.

most detestable

your course of life let natural justice be blamed or called into question

Christian faith

6th-century Greek philosopher

was attracted to or influenced by   animals causing fatal injuries were commonly tried and executed

deadly   pass out (of the body)

unholy mother

But he may be standing. In the Berliner Ensemble production at the Edinburgh Festival, Michael Coveney notes Shylock's "adamantine loyalty to the letter of the law is given a chill reality as he stands on one leg in the courtroom, stropping the knife on the sole of the other shoe" (The Observer, 1995).

What are Bassanio and Antonio doing throughout this? Do they listen to Gratiano and Shylock, pay attention to Nerissa and the Duke, or are they using the time to be with each other? Why doesn't Antonio interrupt Gratiano? or is Gratiano uninterruptible?

see note to l.16

Where is Nerissa's focus? Presumably she's concerned with the Duke's reaction, but how does she respond to Gratiano's outburst and Shylock's humiliation of him? Does Gratiano simply walk away? or is he 'put down' by Shylock and only the Duke's reassertion of authority saves face?

close at hand

149-162 The Duke begins to drive the scene again, reading the letter aloud—this gives time for the young doctor to arrive. The letter gives authority to Portia in her new guise and builds up her entrance. This is necessary if we are to accept her sudden new expertise in Venetian law. The letter's prose allows the audience to ready itself once more for the intensity of verse.

on a friendly visit

urgent request to satisfy

beseech you let his lack of years be no impediment to let him lack° a reverend estimation, for I never knew so young a body with so old a head. I leave him to your gracious acceptance, whose trial shall better publish his commendation."°

Enter PORTIA disguised as BALTHAZAR [a doctor of law, with several of the court.]

You hear the learn'd Bellario, what he writes,
And here I take it is the doctor come.
Give me your hand; come you from old Bellario?

PORTIA I did, my lord.

DUKE You are welcome, take your place.
Are you acquainted with the difference°
That holds this present question° in the court?

PORTIA I am informed throughly° of the cause.°
Which is the merchant here and which the Jew?

DUKE Antonio and old Shylock, both stand forth.

PORTIA Is your name Shylock?

SHYLOCK Shylock is my name.

PORTIA Of a strange nature is the suit you follow,
Yet in such rule° that the Venetian law
Cannot impugn you as you do proceed.
[To ANTONIO.] You stand within his danger,° do you not?

ANTONIO Ay, so he says.

PORTIA Do you confess the bond?

ANTONIO I do.

PORTIA Then must the Jew be merciful.

SHYLOCK On what compulsion must I? Tell me that.

PORTIA The quality of mercy is not strained,°
It droppeth as the gentle rain from heaven
Upon the place beneath. It is twice blest:°
It blesseth him that gives and him that takes;
'Tis mightiest in the mightiest, it becomes

deprive him of

performance will demonstrate the qualities I have already praised (in my letter)

163-178 As the Duke finishes reading aloud he sees and greets Portia. Assured that she has come from Bellario, he gives her authority within the court's proceedings. From Portia's entrance to seeing her act takes seven lines, giving us little time to question her guise.

Is her question a necessary deception? could she not guess at Antonio since Bassanio is nearby? Perhaps the courtroom is crowded? Is the play more interesting if Shylock and Antonio are hard to tell apart because it calls racial stereotyping into question?

dispute

case

thoroughly case

In Peter Zadek's Berliner Ensemble production, the stereotypes are reversed. "Portia instinctively concludes that Ignaz Kirchner's Antonio, a small, dark, unprepossessing figure myopically blinking behind his specs is the Jew. Gert Voss's Shylock must, she assumes, be the Christian merchant, for he is a solid, blandish figure who might be on his way to some local Athenaeum. The Jew appears to be the Aryan" (The Times, 1995).

so far in order

power to do harm

The Duke makes a clear distinction in their ages if not looks, which allows Portia to identify Shylock. Is part of the reason Portia focuses first on the Duke, and then Shylock, because she is still growing into her gendered role? If others accept her as a man, then will Bassanio as well?

As Portia begins to address the court, note how she keeps her distance from Antonio, establishing not his name but his situation.

179-203 When she turns to Shylock with an imperative 'must', she sounds all the more coercive. The audience has heard this line of questioning a number of times now, and seen Shylock fending it off. Does the courtroom's heart sink?

subject to constraint, compulsion

grants a double blessing

The Duke and others simply requested 'mercy' but in this speech Portia opens out the implications, appealing to a common sense of religion and

The throned monarch better than his crown.
His scepter shows the force of temporal power,
The attribute to° awe and majesty
Wherein doth sit the dread and fear of kings.
But mercy is above this sceptered sway:
It is enthroned in the hearts of kings,
It is an attribute to° God himself,
And earthly power doth then show likest God's
When mercy seasons justice. Therefore, Jew,
Though justice be thy plea, consider this,
That in the course of justice° none of us
Should see salvation. We do pray for mercy,
And that same prayer doth teach us all to render
The deeds of mercy. I have spoke thus much
To mitigate the justice of thy plea,°
Which if thou follow, this strict court of Venice
Must needs give sentence 'gainst the merchant there.

SHYLOCK My deeds upon my head! I crave the law,
The penalty and forfeit of my bond.

PORTIA Is he not able to discharge the money?

BASSANIO Yes, here I tender it for him in the court,
Yea, twice the sum; if that will not suffice,
I will be bound to pay it ten times o'er
On forfeit of my hands, my head, my heart;
If this will not suffice, it must appear
That malice bears down° truth. And I beseech you
Wrest once the law to your authority;°
To do a great right, do a little wrong,
And curb this cruel devil of his will.

PORTIA It must not be. There is no power in Venice
Can alter a decree established.
'Twill be recorded for a precedent,
And many an error by the same example
Will rush into the state. It cannot be.

SHYLOCK A Daniel come to judgement, yea a Daniel!°
O wise young judge, how I do honor thee.

PORTIA I pray you, let me look upon the bond.

how little earthly power is by comparison. Although the whole courtroom's attention is directed at Shylock, Portia is not confrontational. She gives Shylock a vision to contextualise a change of heart.

of

The religious force of the speech, with all its Biblical references and echoes, is difficult to reproduce today. The emphasis has to be on its ability to persuade. Yet it's an uneasy persuasion to listen to, since we have heard many of the verbal echoes before. Shylock simply rejects Portia's plea.

of

i.e. justice alone, untempered by mercy

to moderate your plea for rigid justice

204-220 Portia moves on to money and the bond; which we have heard before, and it was ineffective. As Portia goes through these options, Antonio, the Duke and others know this will go nowhere. Does a mood of depression grow within the courtroom? At this point Portia asks a question Bassanio answers, and he doesn't recognise her. Might Nerissa intrude herself to show the tension of disguise?

overpowers

for once subject the law to your (personal) authority

Does 'Bassanio' offer himself because he knows Shylock will reject more money? Is Portia impressed or horrified by this? Bassanio pleads with Portia to save Antonio by depriving Shylock of the law. Since neither she nor anyone interrupts him, does Shylock show worry? He has entertained the possibility of this denial himself. Does this fear strengthen Shylock's resolve by his being pushed to extremes? In the event Portia upholds the law and Shylock's celebratory outburst shows a renewed confidence.

in the Apocrypha's History of Susannah, Daniel is a young judge who saves Susannah from her false accusers

221-230 Is Portia improvising when she overrides

SHYLOCK Here 'tis, most reverend° doctor, here it is.

PORTIA Shylock, there's thrice thy money offered thee.

SHYLOCK An oath, an oath, I have an oath in heaven.
Shall I lay perjury upon my soul?
No, not for Venice.

PORTIA Why, this bond is forfeit,
And lawfully by this the Jew may claim
A pound of flesh, to be by him cut off
Nearest the merchant's heart. Be merciful,
Take thrice thy money, bid me tear the bond.

SHYLOCK When it is paid, according to the tenor.°
It doth appear you are a worthy judge,
You know the law, your exposition
Hath been most sound. I charge you by the law,
Whereof you are a well-deserving pillar,
Proceed to judgement. By my soul I swear
There is no power in the tongue of man
To alter me. I stay here on my bond.

ANTONIO Most heartily I do beseech the court
To give the judgement.

PORTIA Why then thus it is:
You must prepare your bosom for his knife—

SHYLOCK O noble judge, O excellent young man!

PORTIA —For the intent and purpose of the law
Hath full relation to° the penalty,
Which here appeareth due upon the bond.

SHYLOCK 'Tis very true. O wise and upright judge,
How much more elder art thou than thy looks.

PORTIA Therefore lay bare your bosom.

SHYLOCK Ay, his breast,
So says the bond, doth it not noble judge?
"Nearest the heart," those are the very words.

PORTIA It is so. Are there balance° here to weigh the flesh?

SHYLOCK I have them ready.

worthy

Shylock's exultation and asks to read the bond? The trial begins to move forward. Shylock is as eager to give her the bond as Bassanio was to give money, and she manipulates her new reputation for even-handedness by balancing the two. Before beginning to read the bond Portia ups the ante to three times the money lent which, incongruously, also has the effect of making Antonio's case look more hopeless. Shylock in line 224 echoes the cadences of 3.1 by almost crying like a wounded animal.

We may have assumed Antonio's case was hopeless, and Portia's reading of the bond seems to ensure that this is the case. Yet the effect of this new development was to raise our hopes in order to dash them.

precise conditions

231-249 Shylock emerges from the development resolute, tough, courteous and in control of his language.

With each of Portia's examinations failing to break new ground Antonio must feel the mounting pressure. He too now asks for the case to come to a judgment. Note how tension and humour is created through submerged wordplay: Shylock's 'no power in the tongue of man' and Antonio's 'most heartily'.

Is the scene more interesting if Portia is constantly living off her wits? improvising to find a way through? Yet there is a finality in the phrasing of her line 'Why then it is thus' that signifies a conclusion. Portia's judgment fluctuates between layman's language and that of the law. Throughout she allows Shylock to interject, as if she is buying time. Shylock is getting excited, reciting exact phrasings from the bond as if in the grip of an obsession.

fully authorizes

250-257 Portia continues to buy time by exploring the ramifications of the judgment: the scales recall the butcher, as well as those of justice. Does Shylock show them?

As tension builds on stage once more Portia delays by asking for a surgeon. The request suggests desperation. Antonio is clear he will die. Portia's concern for a surgeon sends out another probe for a compassionate chink in Shylock's armour. Shylock insists that Portia look for this in the bond, and because it is not there, says 'no'. The actor Macklin delivered this with a 'savage sneer', Kean with a 'chuckle', and just as plausible would be cool detachment, hysterical crowing: but all reactions show his implacability.

scales

PORTIA Have by some surgeon, Shylock, on your charge°
To stop his wounds, lest he do bleed to death.

SHYLOCK Is it so nominated in the bond?

PORTIA It is not so expressed, but what of that?
'Twere good you do so much for charity.

SHYLOCK I cannot find it, 'tis not in the bond.

PORTIA You, merchant, have you anything to say?

ANTONIO But little. I am armed° and well prepared.
Give me your hand, Bassanio; fare you well.
Grieve not that I am fall'n to this for you,
For herein fortune shows herself more kind
Than is her custom: it is still her use°
To let the wretched man outlive his wealth
To view with hollow eye and wrinkled brow
An age of poverty, from which lingering penance
Of such misery doth she cut me off.
Commend me to your honorable wife,
Tell her the process° of Antonio's end,
Say how I loved you, speak me fair in° death;
And when the tale is told, bid her be judge
Whether Bassanio had not once a love.°
Repent but you° that you shall lose your friend,
And he repents not that he pays your debt,
For if the Jew do cut but deep enough,
I'll pay it instantly with all my heart.

BASSANIO Antonio, I am married to a wife
Which is as dear to me as life itself,
But life itself, my wife, and all the world
Are not with me esteemed above thy life.
I would lose all, ay, sacrifice them all
Here to this devil, to deliver you.

PORTIA Your wife would give you little thanks for that
If she were by to hear you make the offer.°

GRATIANO I have a wife who I protest I love;
I would she were in heaven, so she could
Entreat some power to change this currish Jew.

at your expense

i.e. mentally fortified

always her practice

story

speak well of the manner of my

true friend

regret only (same sense next line)

perhaps spoken as an aside, and]or to Nerissa

258-269 Portia moves the process forward, shifting focus to Antonio. Instead of speaking to the court, Antonio takes leave of Bassanio. Do they shake hands? or is it emotional—'affection wondrous sensible/He wrung Bassanio's hand' as Solanio describes in 2.8? In these moments before his death Antonio is clear-headed, able to marshall his arguments, and it is he who gives Bassanio courage. Does he talk a good show? or is he resolved? Antonio asks to be remembered to Portia, a timely reminder that she is there on stage, for the intensity of the action may well have erased the sense of doubleness that runs through the scene.

270-292 It is possible to play these lines as a love scene, given Antonio's elaboration on the singular and complete love for the paramount friend, and that he only speaks to Bassanio and nobody else. Do they kiss?

Bassanio replies with his own declaration of love for Antonio, which contrasts his 'wife' with the intimacy and definitiveness of his 'friend'. Portia's presence gives edge to the dialogue. In Peter Sellar's production at the Goodman Theatre in Chicago (1994), Antonio loves Bassanio with a passion unmatched by any other love in the play. Michael Billington observed: “Portia is torn apart by the realisation that all her money can't compete with Bassanio's bisexuality: she looks on amazed as her husband slobbers over Antonio in the trial scene” (The Guardian, 1994.b).

Portia's sardonic ourtburst breaks the edge with the comedic. Is it hard for her to defend Antonio while watching their love? Tension having been broken, it can be piled up once again. Portia's line is an interjection, and Antonio, Bassanio and Gratiano may not even hear it.

Gratiano's speech appears to follow on from Bassanio, except that it too is comedic in trying to outdo Bassanio's feelings. Once more Gratiano is responsible for continuing the current of hatred for Jews that flows through the play.

Nerissa interjects, just like Portia, and keeps the comedy alive. What are Bassanio and Antonio doing through these exchanges? Is Antonio in the well of the court, unbuttoning his clothes? readying his breast for the knife.

Given the way both Bassanio and Gratiano are so ready to sacrifice their wives, Shylock would rather see his daughter with a Jewish thief than a

NERISSA 'Tis well you offer it behind her back,
The wish would make else an unquiet house.°

SHYLOCK These be the Christian husbands. I have a daughter:
Would any of the stock of Barabbas°
Had been her husband, rather than a Christian.
We trifle time; I pray thee pursue° sentence.

PORTIA A pound of that same merchant's flesh is thine.
The court awards it, and the law doth give it.

SHYLOCK Most rightful judge.

PORTIA And you must cut this flesh from off his breast.
The law allows it, and the court awards it.

SHYLOCK Most learned judge. A sentence: come, prepare.

PORTIA Tarry a little, there is something else.
This bond doth give thee here no jot of blood.
The words expressly are "a pound of flesh."
Take then thy bond, take thou thy pound of flesh;
But in the cutting it, if thou dost shed
One drop of Christian blood, thy lands and goods
Are by the laws of Venice confiscate
Unto the state of Venice.

GRATIANO O upright judge! Mark, Jew. O learned judge!

SHYLOCK Is that the law?

PORTIA Thyself shalt see the act,
For as thou urgest justice, be assured
Thou shalt have justice more than thou desir'st.

GRATIANO O learned judge! Mark, Jew, a learned judge.

SHYLOCK I take this° offer, then. Pay the bond thrice
And let the Christian go.

BASSANIO Here is the money.

PORTIA Soft.° The Jew shall have all° justice. Soft, no haste.
He shall have nothing but the penalty.

GRATIANO O Jew, an upright judge, a learned judge!

PORTIA Therefore prepare thee to cut off the flesh.

Christian husband. The speech is an indication of how far he has moved from loving his daughter, and humanity in general.

perhaps spoken as an aside, and/or to Portia

1) the thief released by Pontius Pilate in place of Jesus 2) the villain-hero of Christopher's Marlowe's Jew of Malta; stress on the first syllable

proceed to the

293-307 Shylock tires of Portia's delays, and she responds with legal rigamarole. She's clearly stalling, nothing is new, and after Shylock's rather curt praise of her in line 296, there are six silent beats as she flounders. Is this the moment she begins to understand a way out of the situation? and does she continue in her holding pattern for the next two lines while she reads the bond again?

Shylock has insisted on the literal tenor of the bond, and from that she finds the way forward. "With his knife clenched between his teeth in a parody of Christian violence, Dustin Hoffman's Shylock has the last laugh" (Daily Express, 1989). But note, she does so only by taking on Shylock's point of view. Her new judgment is delivered with no hesitation (ll. 304-307).

308-314 Gratiano literally pays Shylock back, mimicking his interruptions of Portia's earlier judgment, and calling 'Mark Jew' as if he is getting Shylock to watch him play 'Shylock'. His question 'Is that the law?' returns him from his private, literal reading of the bond as the only law, to the larger laws of Venice which he thought he had under control.

There's bitter irony in line 311: it can mean 'because you ask for justice' or 'in the manner you ask for justice', that is, without mercy. Is Shylock's response directly to Bassanio? for Bassanio quickly delivers the money before Shylock changes his mind.

315-328 There must be a flurry of action since Portia takes two full lines to bring the situation under control. Despite Gratiano's interjections, Portia carries on as if it's one speech. Does she insist that Shylock pick up the knife and Antonio continue to bare his breast?

i.e. Portia's offer of triple payment, l.230 (or perhaps Bassanio's offer of double money, l.206—the inconsistency is of no consequence in performance)

wait   all nothing but

In many productions Antonio is pinioned in his chair or held on the floor, for example, in David Thacker's production for the RSC in 1994. This was taken further in the earlier 1988 production with Antony Sher: "The trial scene thus becomes Shylock's apotheosis. Brandishing a dagger, ranging the scales and blood-spattered towel in front of the pinioned Antonio, chanting in a ritual revenge, Sher is mesmerised like some predatory animal poised for

Shed thou no blood, nor cut thou less nor more
But just a pound of flesh. If thou tak'st more
Or less than a just° pound, be it but so much
As makes it light or heavy in the substance°
Or the division° of the twentieth part
Of one poor scruple°—nay, if the scale do turn
But in the estimation° of a hair,
Thou diest and all thy goods are confiscate.

GRATIANO A second Daniel, a Daniel, Jew!
Now, infidel, I have you on the hip.°

PORTIA Why doth the Jew pause? Take thy forfeiture.

SHYLOCK Give me my principal and let me go.

BASSANIO I have it ready for thee, here it is.

PORTIA He hath refused it in the open court.
He shall have merely° justice and his bond.

GRATIANO A Daniel, still say I, a second Daniel!
I thank thee, Jew, for teaching me that word.

SHYLOCK Shall I not have barely my principal?

PORTIA Thou shalt have nothing but the forfeiture
To be so taken at thy peril, Jew.

SHYLOCK Why, then, the devil give him good of it.
I'll stay no longer question.°

PORTIA Tarry, Jew,
The law hath yet another hold on you.
It is enacted in the laws of Venice,
If it be proved against an alien
That by direct or indirect attempts
He seek the life of any citizen,
The party 'gainst the which he doth contrive
Shall seize one half his goods, the other half
Comes to the privy coffer° of the state,
And the offender's life lies in the mercy
Of the Duke only, 'gainst all other voice.°
In which predicament I say thou stand'st,
For it appears by manifest proceeding

the kill" (The Guardian, 1988).

exact
weight
portion
20 grains
weight or fraction

As Portia interprets the wording of the bond ever more precisely, she turns Shylock's language against him. If there is relief in Antonio's corner, there is still a sense of alarm in case Shylock plunges the knife in. Gratiano too echoes Shylock's language yet the taunting adds tension: mights he kill Antonio in response?

at my mercy (compare I.iii.39)

329-340 Shylock doesn't know which way to turn. Is line 330 whispered defeat? Bassanio's understanding of Portia's strategy is to bargain Shylock down to the original sum. Portia is resolute and repeats her command.

strictly

In Jude Kelly's 1994 production for the West Yorkshire Playhouse "she stills urges Shylock to 'Prepare thee to cut off the flesh' not without a spasm of malice against Antonio." (Financial Times, 1994). Throughout these lines Shylock increasingly doesn't know where to turn, and asks for money a third time, only to have Portia refuse anything but the forfeit. Shylock realises debate is useless and prepares to go.

dispute the case no longer

341-357 Portia orders him to stay. And here the scene moves into a different area again. As much as Venetian society might want to punish Shylock because he is a Jew, by its charter it cannot. But in terms of the play it can convict him as a threatening alien.

To accomplish this delicate manoeuvre the nature of Shylock's difference is reconstituted: a Jew at the start of the speech, three lines later he is an alien. Yet once Shylock is convicted as an alien, he can be punished, not as an alien, but as a Jew, who must 'presently become a Christian...'. James Shapiro in his Shakespeare and the Jews develops this idea at length.

private treasury (for the monarch's personal expenses, like the English Privy Purse)

with no possibility of appeal

If Portia has this information before ever going into the courtroom then why does she go through the whole procedure? is it to test Shylock? to discover the depth of feeling between Bassanio and Antonio? Perhaps the scene is necessary precisely so that Shylock can be shown to be a threat to the citizenry. Does the passion and obsession he displays put him beyond humanity as Venice knows it? Or is this scene best staged as one which shows the limits of Venice, the way that all cultures have blank spots, areas they simply do not understand, and that these become their failings?

That indirectly, and directly too,
Thou hast contrived against the very life
Of the defendant, and thou hast incurred
The danger formerly by me rehearsed.°
Down, therefore, and beg mercy of the Duke.

GRATIANO Beg that thou mayst have leave to hang thyself.
And yet thy wealth being forfeit to the state,
Thou hast not left the value of a cord,
Therefore thou must be hanged at the state's charge.

DUKE That thou shalt see the difference of our° spirit,
I pardon thee thy life before thou ask it.
For° half thy wealth, it is Antonio's,
The other half comes to the general state,
Which humbleness may drive unto° a fine.

PORTIA Ay, for the state, not for Antonio.°

SHYLOCK Nay, take my life and all, pardon not that.
You take my house when you do take the prop
That doth sustain my house; you take my life
When you do take the means whereby I live.

PORTIA What mercy can you render him, Antonio?

GRATIANO A halter° gratis, nothing else, for God's sake.

ANTONIO So please my lord the duke and all the court
To quit° the fine for one half of his goods,
I am content, so° he will let me have
The other half in use° to render it
Upon his death unto the gentleman
That lately stole his daughter.
Two things provided more: that for this favor
He presently° become a Christian;
The other, that he do record a gift°
Here in the court of all he dies possessed
Unto his son° Lorenzo and his daughter.

DUKE He shall do this, or else I do recant°
The pardon that I late pronounced here.

PORTIA Art thou contented, Jew? What dost thou say?

Whether it is one or another partly depends on how Gratiano's counterpoint is staged: is it the petty chatter of a minor character who shows up the dignity of the court? or is it the popular voice running parallel with the court's decisions, the true heart of Venice?

stage legalese: "the penalty I have already cited"

Note Portia's legalistic vocabulary as she orders Shylock to kneel to the Duke. Although reversing his earlier words, she is echoing Shylock's refusal of mercy.

358-371 Gratiano's brutal speech keeps Shylock on his knees the longer, and here provides a contrast with the more forgiving and merciful dignitaries of the court. The Duke's judgment can be misunderstood, so Portia is quick to clarify that Antonio is left free to 'render mercy' with his portion. Shylock sees the loss of his 'house', both residence and family, and the means of earning his living, as a death sentence.

see note to l 16

as for

humble behavior may reduce to

In her judicial role, Portia underlines the legal detail in the Duke's sentence

However, in Peter Zadek's Berliner Ensemble production; Shylock was played as an assimilated Jew. Paul Taylor says "When ordered by the court to give half his goods to his victim and half to the state, Gert Voss's Shylock promptly kneels down and, pressing against the floor, writes out two cheques in a breathtakingly calm, orderly fashion, glancing at his watch to check the date." (The Independent, 1995).

372-387 Shylock's complaint highlights his earlier lack of compassion, and sharpens the difference between the two as Antonio shows mercy. At this point Gratiano's interjections mean little, no one listens. Is he now the distanced and unacceptable face of Venice?

noose

remit

providing

in trust

However much Antonio may have sounded like Gratiano earlier, here he behaves generously. When he says that he will take his half share of Shylock's estate and invest it on behalf of Lorenzo and Jessica, he is firmly underlining his rejection of usury; while emphasising that his investments will be in 'ventures'.

immediately

deed of gift

Paradoxically, by saying that Lorenzo 'stole' Shylock's daughter, thereby indicating his own approval and making himself complicit in the theft, Antonio points up that harshness is not only one sided.

son-in-law

retract

Line 379 has seven beats. What happens to Shylock in the silence? Are Antonio's next five lines an afterthought? What gives Antonio the right to

SHYLOCK I am content.

PORTIA Clerk, draw a deed of gift.

SHYLOCK I pray you give me leave to go from hence,
I am not well. Send the deed after me
And I will sign it.

DUKE Get thee gone, but do it.

GRATIANO In christ'ning shalt thou have two godfathers.
Had I been judge, thou shouldst have had ten more,°
To bring thee to the gallows, not to the font.°

Exit [SHYLOCK.]

DUKE [To PORTIA.] Sir, I entreat you home with me to dinner.

PORTIA I humbly do desire your grace of pardon,
I must away this night toward Padua,
And it is meet I presently set forth.

DUKE I am sorry that your leisure serves you not.
Antonio, gratify° this gentleman,
For in my mind you are much bound to him.

Exit DUKE and his train.

add two further conditions? Does the silence alert the audience to this transgression?

Line 381 has widely been interpreted as merciful, it means Shylock can now be saved. But becoming a Christian is elsewhere shown as a punishment for Jews, see Marlowe's Jew of Malta. The second condition forces Shylock to approve of Jessica's marriage despite his anger and grief. The Duke embraces these conditions and by the state's power of life, makes Shylock convert by force. David Nathan comments on playing Shylock as a stage villain in the 1998 Shakespeare's Globe production: "Another unhappy aspect of this production is that for the first time in my memory the forced conversion of Shylock and his sudden collapse is greeted with laughter" (Jewish Chronicle, 1998).

i.e. for a trial by twelve "godfathers," the colloquial name for "members of a jury"

i.e. the "christ'ning" or baptismal font

In the RSC production of 1997 Paul Taylor notes "Shylock's humiliation is signalled by the fact that, attempting to rise to his feet to leave the court, he keeps falling back to his knees on the slippery carpet of gold coins contempuously flung down for him earlier." (The Independent, 1997).

David Nathan reviewing the earlier Dustin Hoffman production says "Curiously, there is not even a spasmodic blaze of anger at his forced conversion, and he goes to his fate unprotestingly, hustled out of the court by the gentry and clearly destined for a beating; an ordinary little man who thought he could take on Venice and found he had overreached himself" (Jewish Chronicle, 1989).

reward

Lydia Conway sees the same moment in an entirely different way: "Where this production does come into its own is the effect the trial has on Shylock. It is not the stripping of the assets that breaks him, nor the demand that he become a Christian, nor that his money go to his daughter and Christian son-in-law, but that he has been shown mercy at the hands of the detestable barbarians posing as Christians." (What's On, 1989).

388-395 Shylock feels ill throughout this scene of new conditions. Many actors have played him as a broken man, humiliated and near to death. It's a mystery "why Shylock stays to listen to Gratiano's next three lines. Is this a deliberate and vindictive humiliation which creates sympathy by reminding us of the real attitude of Venice? Is Shylock packing his scales? or is Gratiano preventing him from leaving court? Does Gratiano follow him as he leaves?

On Shylock's exit in the RSC's 1997 pro-

BASSANIO Most worthy gentleman, I and my friend
Have by your wisdom been this day acquitted
Of grievous penalties, in lieu whereof°
Three thousand ducats due unto the Jew
We freely cope° your courteous pains withal.

ANTONIO And stand indebted over and above,
In love and service to you evermore.

PORTIA He is well paid that is well satisfied,
And I, delivering you, am satisfied,
And therein do account myself well paid.
My mind was never yet° more mercenary.
I pray you know° me when we meet again.
I wish you well, and so I take my leave.

BASSANIO Dear sir, of force I must attempt° you further.
Take some remembrance of us as a tribute,
Not as fee. Grant me two things, I pray you:
Not to deny me, and to pardon me.

PORTIA You press me far, and therefore I will yield.
[To ANTONIO.] Give me your gloves, I'll wear them for your sake,
[To BASSANIO.] And for your love I'll take this ring from you.
Do not draw back your hand, I'll take no more,
And you in love° shall not deny my this.

BASSANIO This ring, good sir? Alas, it is a trifle.
I will not shame myself to give you this.

PORTIA I will have nothing else but only this,
And now methinks I have a mind to it.

BASSANIO There's more depends° on this than on the value.
The dearest° ring in Venice will I give you,
And find it out by proclamation,°
Only for this I pray you pardon me.

PORTIA I see, sir, you are liberal in offers.
You taught me first to beg, and now methinks
You teach me how a beggar should be answered.

BASSANIO Good sir, this ring was given me by my wife,
And when she put it on, she made me vow
That I should neither sell, nor give, nor lose it.

duction, Philip Voss "totters out, hands shielding his now uncovered head as if to assert the Jewish identity of which he's been deprived." (Evening Standard, 1997).

The New Cambridge edition cites Kean's withering stare at Gratiano was an important part of his effective exit. Inspired perhaps by the Victorian critics' belief that Shylock is about to die, Irving went out a broken man. Another actor went out bleeding to death from a self-inflicted stab-wound. Olivier uttered a terrible off-stage howl. Whatever the actor playing Shylock does, the motif of Gratiano's insistent brutality and racism leaves any sense that justice has been done in question.

396-419 From now to the end of the scene, the whole process is one of relief, satisfaction, unwinding, celebration, packing up. Humour surfaces for Antonio is 'bound' again, this time to Portia.

This part of the scene makes us aware again of the love interest between Portia and Bassanio. Antonio and Bassanio speak for each other, interchangeably. Portia replies to them interchangeably.

420-443 The language of the sexual double entendre emphasises the doubleness that her disguise has brought to the entire scene, and frames her own uneasiness. She continues to treat Antonio and Bassanio as a couple.

The West Yorkshire Playhouse production took this further. Alastair Macauly comments: "The nastiest shock occurs at the end of this scene. Antonio and her husband treating her as 'one of us' rush upon her with instant talk of love—as if to initiate her into a gay mafia." (Financial Times, 1994).

When she finally accepts their offer of thanks, and asks for the ring, she has seen enough of their relationship to begin testing Bassanio. At this point Bassanio has to begin to reassert the importance of his relationship with Portia, which he does by appealing to her understanding, as she appealed to Shylock's.

Portia presses and presses Bassanio. The ring becomes a test of his love in the real sense. Is Portia trying to gauge whether his relationship with Antonio reflects a general tendency to inconstancy in Bassanio? The situation is a stand-off.

in return for which

requite

not now nor ever before

1) consider ourselves introduced 2) recognize 3) have carnal knowledge of

urge

polite gratitude

at stake

most valuable

public advertisement

PORTIA That 'scuse serves many men to save their gifts;
And if your wife be not a mad woman,
And know how well I have deserved this ring,
She would not hold out° enemy for ever
For giving it to me. Well, peace be with you.

Exeunt [PORTIA and NERISSA.]

ANTONIO My lord Bassanio, let him have the ring.
Let his deservings and my love withal
Be valued 'gainst your wife's commandement.°

BASSANIO Go, Gratiano, run and overtake him,
Give him the ring and bring him if thou canst
Unto Antonio's house. Away, make haste. Exit GRATIANO.
Come, you and I will thither presently,
And in the morning early will we both
Fly toward Belmont. Come, Antonio. Exeunt.

Scene ii Enter [PORTIA and] NERISSA [still disguised.]

PORTIA Inquire the Jew's house out, give him this deed,
And let him sign it. We'll away tonight
And be a day before our husbands home.
This deed will be welcome to Lorenzo.

Enter GRATIANO.

GRATIANO Fair sir, you are well o'erta'en.°
My lord Bassanio upon more advice
Hath sent you here this ring, and doth entreat
Your company at dinner.

PORTIA That cannot be.
His ring I do accept most thankfully,
And so I pray you tell him. Furthermore,
I pray you show my youth old Shylock's house.

GRATIANO That will I do.

444-452 Once Portia leaves, Antonio, who has been sensitive enough not to undermine Bassanio publicly, urges him to give her the ring, even elevating his status to 'Lord Bassanio'. Bassanio cannot hold out against Antonio's pleading. He sends Gratiano with the ring.

remain your

Bassanio begins to organise Antonio - another indication how their relationship has changed. He is no longer dependent on Antonio financially. There's an emotional shift. Antonio may even be slightly bemused, if not dumbfounded, at Bassanio's new-found authority. Has he guessed at it in calling him 'Lord'? Is it significant that despite assuring Portia he would return to Belmont without delay, Bassanio here proposes to spend the night at Antonio's?

(extra syllable for the sake of the meter)

Scene ii

1-20 We catch Portia and Nerissa walking in the street. Portia expects to be home soon, bringing Belmont back to our minds. Gratiano overtakes them, recovering his breath in the short line 5. Portia takes the ring. Given Gratiano's conduct during the trial there is black humour in asking him to conduct Nerissa to Shylock's door.

Receiving the ring is bittersweet: what Portia couldn't make Bassanio do, Antonio can. What kind of hold does Antonio have over her husband? Nerissa speaks to Portia out of Gratiano's hearing and shows solidarity by vowing to get Gratiano's ring. This returns them to the familiar jesting language of 1.2 and 3.4, and helps to distance the high drama of the trial. But why should Gratiano give it up to the lawyer's clerk? Unlike Portia, Nerissa gets it on her own accord. Nerissa and Gratiano leave in one direction, Portia in another.

i.e. fortunately I've caught up with you

NERISSA Sir, I would speak with you.
[Aside to PORTIA.] I'll see if I can get my husband's ring
Which I did make him swear to keep forever.

PORTIA Thou mayst, I warrant. We shall have old° swearing
That they did give the rings away to men,
But we'll outface° them, and outswear them too.
Away, make haste, thou know'st where I will tarry.

NERISSA [To GRATIANO.] Come, good sir, will you show me to this house? [Exeunt.]

plenty of

shame

ACT V

Scene i Enter LORENZO and JESSICA.

LORENZO The moon shines bright. In such a night as this,
When the sweet wind did gently kiss the trees
And they did make no noise, in such a night
Troilus° methinks mounted the Trojan walls
And sighed his soul toward the Grecian tents
Where Cressid lay that night.

JESSICA In such a night
Did Thisbe° fearfully o'ertrip the dew,
And saw the lion's shadow° ere himself,
And ran dismayed away.

LORENZO In such a night
Stood Dido° with a willow° in her hand
Upon the wild sea banks, and waft° her love
To come again to Carthage.

JESSICA In such a night
Medea° gathered the enchanted herbs
That did renew old Aeson.

LORENZO In such a night
Did Jessica steal° from the wealthy Jew,
And with an unthrift° love did run from Venice
As far as Belmont.

JESSICA In such a night
Did young Lorenzo swear he loved her well,
Stealing her soul with many vows of faith,
And ne'er a true one.

LORENZO In such a night

ACT V. Scene i

1-24 Unusually this scene starts at the beginning. As lovers, Lorenzo and Jessica have time to look at the cloudless night, the nearly full moon. They smell the wind, their words sexual, yet each uses examples of unhappy and lonely lovers to the other.

Are these examples of unhappy lovers set off against their own happiness? or are they expressions of fear of parting? Is the verse a sign of formality and playfulness? Are they walking close together, or apart? Each builds the other's story of another love affair, and of the same length. They are clearly attuned to each other, enjoying the imaginative give and take.

At line 12 Jessica changes the story away from lovers to daughters and fathers, and significantly shortens the story by one line. Does she falter? Shylock springs immediately to Lorenzo's mind. Does Jessica play on Aason and 'a son', as Lorenzo will be renamed by Portia's letter?

Lorenzo restores the story to its previous length, and combines lovers with fathers and daughters, narrowing the focus to themselves. Note the play on 'steal', and 'unthrift love'. Does this apply to Lorenzo's love before meeting Jessica? or might it also be the reason why they are in Belmont? Are they speaking to each other about their feelings through telling stories? Does 'Stealing the soul with many vows of faith' also becomes a comment on Jessica's conversion to Christianity?

Lorenzo picks up on the change in rhythm. This speech is shorter than previous ones, and he end stops it, breaking down the synchronicity with Jessica and their play together. Here the scene changes. Jessica hears a man and then falls silent until line 68. Does she absent herself?

Trojan prince forsaken by his lover Cressida after she was sent to the Greek camp in an exchange of prisoners; they were, respectively, the types of faithful and unfaithful lovers

was frightened away by a lion after arranging to meet her lover Pyramus. He found her blood-stained garment, concluded she was dead, and killed himself

i.e. cast by moonlight

Queen of Carthage was abandoned by her lover Aeneas, hero of Virgil's *Aeneid* a symbol of forsaken love

beckoned

a sorceress who rejuvenated Aeson, father of Jason, after helping Jason win the Golden Fleece (see I.iii.169, III.ii.240). He later deserted her

1) steal away 2) rob

spendthrift

Did pretty Jessica, like a little shrew,
Slander her love, and he forgave it her.

JESSICA I would out-night you did nobody come,
But hark, I hear the footing° of a man.

Enter [STEPHANO] a messenger.

LORENZO Who comes so fast in silence of the night?

STEPHANO A friend.

LORENZO A friend? What friend? Your name, I pray you, friend?

STEPHANO Stephano is my name, and I bring word
My mistress will before the break of day
Be here at Belmont. She doth stray about
By holy crosses° where she kneels and prays
For happy wedlock hours.

LORENZO Who comes with her?

STEPHANO None but a holy hermit and her maid.
I pray you, is my master yet returned?

LORENZO He is not, nor we have not heard from him.
But go we in I pray thee, Jessica,
And ceremoniously let us prepare
Some welcome for the mistress of the house.

Enter [LAUNCELOT the] clown.

LAUNCELOT Sola,° sola! Wo ha, ho! Sola, sola!

LORENZO Who calls?

LAUNCELOT Sola! Did you see Master Lorenzo? [Calls.] Master Lorenzo! Sola, sola!

LORENZO Leave hollering, man. Here!

LAUNCELOT Sola!—where, where?

LORENZO Here!

LAUNCELOT Tell him there's a post° come from my master, with his horn full of good news:° my master will be here ere morning.

[Exit.]

footsteps

25-38 Or is she left behind by Lorenzo? Line 26 suggests eight silent beats for Lorenzo to find the messenger. Has the servant been renamed Stephano because Portia has yet to unravel her identity as Balthazar? Stephano's answer about the hermit, and his following question remind us of Portia's excuse for leaving Belmont. Lorenzo's 'I pray thee Jessica' suggests her reluctance to go in.

stop intermittently at wayside crosses

Launcelot imitates the sound of a hunting horn

39-47 They are interrupted by Launcelot, pretending he cannot see Lorenzo despite the bright moonlight. Given the play would originally have been performed during daylight and that the scene is set at night-time when the moon is bright, is this underwritten scene an excuse for Launcelot to fool around with night in day?

Launcelot continues his hunting calls, hearing the voice but not recognising it. Then, recognising Lorenzo's voice, he pretends he can't see him. Lorenzo leaves this behind though Launcelot always frustrates him.

messenger

a pun on the literal meaning of cornucopia, "horn of plenty"

LORENZO Sweet soul, let's in, and there expect° their coming.
And yet no matter, why should we go in?
My friend Stephano, signify, I pray you,
Within the house your mistress is at hand,
And bring your music forth into the air. [Exit STEPHANO.]
How sweet the moonlight sleeps upon this bank.
Here will we sit, and let the sounds of music
Creep in our ears; soft stillness and the night
Become the touches° of sweet harmony.
Sit, Jessica. Look how the floor of heaven
Is thick inlaid with patens° of bright gold.
There's not the smallest orb which thou behold'st
But in his motion° like an angel sings,
Still choiring to the young-eyed cherubins.°
Such harmony is in immortal souls,
But whilst this muddy vesture° of decay
Doth grossly° close it in, we cannot hear it.°

[Enter STEPHANO and MUSICIANS.]

Come, ho, and wake Diana° with a hymn.
With sweet touches pierce your mistress' ear,
And draw her home with music. [Play music.]

JESSICA I am never merry when I hear sweet music.

LORENZO The reason is your spirits are attentive,°
For do but note a wild and wanton° heard
Or race° of youthful and unhandled colts,
Fetching mad bounds,° bellowing and neighing loud,
Which is the hot condition of their blood:°
If they but hear perchance a trumpet sound,
Or any air of music touch their ears,
You shall perceive them make a mutual° stand,
Their savage eyes turned to a modest gaze,
By the sweet power of music. Therefore the poet°
Did feign° that Orpheus drew trees, stones, and floods,
Since naught so stockish,° hard, and full of rage
But music for the time° doth change his nature.
The man that hath no music in himself
Nor is not moved with concord of sweet sounds,
Is fit for treasons, strategems, and spoils;°

await

48-67 Stephano leaves. Lorenzo talks with Jessica as if beginning a new scene. He sits at line 54, yet Jessica still needs coaxing to sit at line 57. He looks at the 'heavens' but has to ask her to look. Lorenzo speaks three times of mythical or biblical portrayals of 'eyes' and then of the unheard 'harmony' of the soul. At this, musicians enter. It is as if Jessica is unreachable. With 'draw her home with music' Lorenzo wants Jessica's spirit to come back to the present.

suit the notes (produced at the touch of an instrument)

shallow gold or silver dish holding the host at celebrations of the Eucharist; may also refer to gilded bosses at the joins of roof-vaulting

its motion (which was thought to produce music)

an order of angels

i.e. mortal body (which God created from wet earth in Genesis 2:6-7)

materially i.e. music produced by the motion of the spheres cannot be heard by human ears

goddess of the moon

68-87 Once the music starts, Jessica speaks for the first time in 45 lines, and the last time in the play. She does seem to return. Lorenzo's reply brings us back to the senses, how body and soul listen to music. He is trying to explain to Jessica both her aloneness and connectedness. His explanation is marked by the sexual energy conveyed by music and his motif of horses, untamed, possessed, in 'the hot condition of their blood'.

There is an apocalyptic note in the 'trumpet sound', as if this peculiar speech is partly about Jessica's conversion from 'savage eyes' to 'modest gaze', both by becoming Christian and a wife. Is this 'music' a compensation for losing her father and joining Lorenzo's world?

Lines 85-6 Lorenzo speaks of darkness. Does the moon cloud over?

perceptive faculties are too narrowly focused

frolicsome

charge

making fiery leaps

impulsive temperament characteristic of their youth

common

perhaps Ovid telling the story of Orpheus, who charmed both animate and inanimate objects with his music

relate

nothing so blockish

i.e. while it plays

acts of plunder

The motions of his spirit are dull as night,°
And his affections° dark as Erebus.°
Let no such man be trusted. Mark the music.

Enter PORTIA and NERISSA.

PORTIA That light we see is burning in my hall.
How far that little candle throws his beams;
So shines a good deed in a naughty° world.

NERISSA When the moon shone we did not see the candle.

PORTIA So doth the greater glory dim the less;
A substitute° shines brightly as a king
Until a king be by, and then his° state
Empties° itself, as doth an inland brook
Into the main of waters. Music, hark!

NERISSA It is your music, madam, of the house.

PORTIA Nothing is good, I see, without respect;°
Methinks it sounds much sweeter than by day.

NERISSA Silence bestows that virtue on it, madam.

PORTIA The crow doth sing as sweetly as the lark
When neither is attended,° and I think
The nightingale, if she should sing by day
When every goose is cackling, would be thought
No better a musician than the wren.
How many things by season seasoned are°
To their right praise and true perfection.
Peace.

[Music ceases.]

How the moon sleeps with Endymion,°
And would not be awaked.

LORENZO That is the voice,
Or I am much deceived, of Portia.

PORTIA He knows me as the blind man knows the cuckoo,
By the bad voice.

LORENZO Dear lady, welcome home.

i.e. his impulses are sinister yet hidden

feelings   part of the classical underworld

wicked

deputy

i.e. the substitute's

discharges

a comparative context

either is (heard) alone

a) by proper spicing are b) by being matured brought c) by happening at what is considered to be a favorable time valued

shepherd-lover of the moon goddess Diana, who caused him to sleep perpetually in a cave on Mount Latmos so she could always visit him

88-107 As Portia and Nerissa arrive, they enter into a darker scene. They are distant from the house though close enough to see light inside, highlighting their separation from Lorenzo and Jessica and the musicians.

Their speech continues the heightened language of the scene. At line 96 they hear the music but cannot see the musicians, nor, by inference, Lorenzo or Jessica. Because they are responsive to music, are they to be trusted? Does this tie them to Jessica and her new world?

Lines 101 to 104 promise to disrupt the man-made harmony of music with the day dawning, and the natural cacophany of birds. Portia picks up the shift and shouts 'Peace!'

108-125 With 'Peace!' Portia takes back command of Belmont. The musicians stop playing. Does Portia, in lines 108-109, move over to them and indicate they they should leave? Lorenzo wakens.

Once Portia learns of Bassanio's early return, she sets another train in motion. Despite her command to Nerissa, no exit is given for her. Does she stay because the tucket sounds? Does she run into the house as Gratiano enters? if he runs in after her, do both make a noisy re-entry on line 141?

Surprisingly, Bassanio is the only private

PORTIA We have been praying for our husbands' welfare,
Which° speed, we hope, the better for our words.
Are they returned?

LORENZO Madam, they are not yet,
But there is come a messenger before
To signify their coming.

PORTIA Go in, Nerissa,
Give order to my servants that they take
No note at all of our being absent hence —
Nor you Lorenzo, Jessica nor you. [A tucket° sounds.]

LORENZO Your husband is at hand, I hear his trumpet.
We are no tell-tales, madam, fear you not.

PORTIA This night, methinks, is but the daylight sick,
It looks a little paler; 'tis a day
Such as the day is when the sun is hid.

Enter BASSANIO, ANTONIO, GRATIANO, and their followers.

[GRATIANO and NERISSA talk apart.]

BASSANIO We should hold day with the Antipodes,
If you would walk in absence of the sun.°

PORTIA Let me give light, but let me not be light,°
For a light wife doth make a heavy° husband,
And never be Bassanio so for me.
But God sort° all. You are welcome home, my lord.

BASSANIO I thank you, madam. Give welcome to my friend.
This is the man, this is Antonio,
To whom I am so infinitely bound.

PORTIA You should in all sense° be much bound to him,
For as I hear, he was much bound for you.

ANTONIO No more than I am well acquitted of.°

PORTIA Sir, you are very welcome to our house.
It must appear in other ways than words,
Therefore I scant° this breathing courtesy.

GRATIANO [To NERISSA.] By yonder moon I swear you do me wrong!

who

citizen in Shakespeare to have his own 'tucket'. Does it reinforce his change of status? At its sound, Portia changes the subject abruptly, talks of the weather and appears unconcerned as Bassanio and all enter.

short trumpet flourish

126-140 But this also draws our attention to the breaking of day, everyone can now see each other.

Bassanio has heard Portia speak, and responds as if they are in the middle of a quiet conversation. It not only defuses the buildup of the scene, but conveys to Antonio and all, the feeling that Bassanio is 'home'.

enjoy daylight at the same time as the other side of the globe if you (like a second sun) walk about at night

puns on the senses "be wanton"..."unchaste"

sad

let God dispose

There is irony in Portia's reply—by giving up her ring, Bassanio has made her a 'light' wife. They greet each other warmly, if formally and Bassanio introduces Antonio as his friend. Note that he uses the present tense. Does this indicate to Portia that their relationship will continue? Portia answers with courtesy but in the past tense, and plays with three meanings of the word 'bound': 'indebted', 'pledged', and 'imprisoned'. Throughout these introductions, is Jessica wondering what happened to Shylock? Portia, ever generous, gives welcome.

1) every way 2) all reason

1) repaid for 2) released from

In Peter Sellar's 1994 production we see Antonio and Bassanio kissing each other passionately during the play, the last time being in the courtroom scene. Kate Kellaway mentions "When Portia returns in the dark to welcome Antonio and her husband into her house, you can't help but fear that this is the beginning of a doomed menage a trois" (The Observer, 1994).

cut short this merely verbal welcome

141-168 Nerissa and Gratiano burst into the scene

In faith, I gave it to the judge's clerk;
Would he were gelt° that had it for my part,°
Since you do take it, love, so much at heart.

PORTIA A quarrel ho, already. What's the matter?

GRATIANO About a hoop of gold, a paltry ring
That she did give me, whose posy° was
For all the world like cutler's poetry°
Upon a knife: "Love me, and leave me not."

NERISSA What talk you of the posy or the value?
You swore to me when I did give it you
That you would wear it till your hour of death,
And that it should lie with you in your grave.
Though not for me, yet° for your vehement oaths,
You should have been respective° and have kept it.
Gave it a judge's clerk! No, God's my judge
The clerk will ne'er wear hair on's face that had it.

GRATIANO He will, and if° he live to be a man.

NERISSA Ay, if a woman live to be a man.

GRATIANO Now by this hand, I gave it to a youth,
A kind of boy, a little scrubbed° boy
No higher than thyself, the judge's clerk,
A prating° boy that begged it as a fee;
I could not for my heart deny it him.

PORTIA You were to blame, I must be plain with you,
To part so slightly with your wife's first gift,
A thing stuck on with oaths upon your finger
And so riveted with faith unto your flesh.
I gave my love a ring and made him swear
Never to part with it, and here he stands.
I dare be sworn for him he would not leave it,
Nor pluck it from his finger for the wealth
That the world masters.° Now, in faith, Gratiano,
You give your wife too unkind a cause of grief,
And 'twere to me, I should be mad° at it.

BASSANIO [Aside.] Why, I were best to cut my left hand off,
And swear I lost the ring defending it.

and break up its rhythm. Gratiano swears by the moon which is unpropitious given its continual change and a joke given the moon has disappeared. His play on 'gelt' reminds us of money and castration. Its comedy fits with Nerissa's character as the male clerk. There was no compulsion on Gratiano's part to give the ring, and Nerissa now conveys her hurt through silence, Bassanio must be worried.

gelded 1) as far as I'm concerned 2) on my behalf

inscribed motto

a sneering phrase: "trite verses by a maker of cutlery"

Portia interrupts with an 'innocent' question that gets her own quarrel going. As usual, Gratiano answers guilelessly, providing an index to the undercurrent of real feelings in the group. He betrays any emotional commitment to the ring, belittling its meaning and being intentionally hurtful.

Nerissa ups the stakes and directly challenges Gratiano's story, which, although humourous, warns the audience of the more serious parallel quarrel about to happen. Gratiano's hand is displayed here: he may be stretching it out automatically, only realising its ringlessness afterwards, or Nerissa may be clutching it to display its ringless state.

if…even

mindful (of the circumstances under which it was given)

Do lines 161-163 take her aback, as Gratiano speaks contemptuously and belittlingly of the 'clerk' and the ring? Portia interrupts again, quietening Gratiano and switching the focus to Bassanio.

if

But as she goes hard at Gratiano, what must Bassanio be thinking? Is Bassanio already standing in such a way that his ring hand isn't visible to Portia?

stunted

chattering

169-191 She intensifies the situation by swearing belief in him, and by saying unlike Nerissa she would be possessed by uncontrollable rage. Bassanio slinks into an aside: they can see him but not hear him. It is Gratiano who decides that he has waited long enough and lands Bassanio in it.

owns

As Portia continues to profess belief in Bassanio, does she carry herself as in the courtroom, daring recognition, or as the mistress of Belmont? Bassanio says nothing. Is he trying to think a way through his predicament? Finally he has to speak and confesses by showing his ringless finger.

furious

GRATIANO My lord Bassanio gave his ring away
Unto the judge that begged it, and indeed
Deserved it too; and then the boy his clerk
That took some pains in writing, he begged mine,
And neither man nor master would take aught°
But the two rings.

PORTIA What ring gave you, my lord?
Not that, I hope, which you received of me?

BASSANIO If I could add a lie unto a fault,
I would deny it, but you see my finger
Hath not the ring upon it, it is gone.

PORTIA Even so void is your false heart of truth.
By heaven, I will ne'er come in your bed
Until I see the ring.

NERISSA Nor I in yours,
Till I again see mine.

BASSANIO Sweet Portia,
If you did know to whom I gave the ring,
If you did know for whom I gave the ring,
And would conceive for what I gave the ring,
And how unwillingly I left the ring,
When naught would be accepted but the ring,
You would abate the strength of your displeasure.

PORTIA If you had known the virtue° of the ring,
Or half her worthiness that gave the ring,
Or your own honor to contain° the ring,
You would not then have parted with the ring.
What man is there so much unreasonable
If you had pleased to have defended it
With any terms of zeal,° wanted the modesty
To urge the thing held as a ceremony?°
Nerissa teaches me what to believe:
I'll die for it, but some woman had the ring.

BASSANIO No, by my honor, madam! By my soul
No woman had it, but a civil doctor,°
Which did refuse three thousand ducats of me
And begged the ring, the which I did deny him

Note that Portia doesn't argue, just comments and swears an oath, thereby putting the onus onto Bassanio. Nerissa does the same.

anything

192-207 Bassanio uses the same rhetorical device as at 3.2.256-260—he seems to use this under stress—and it must hurt Portia since it values Antonio over her. Nevertheless, she recognises the strategy for she coolly parodies it (ll. 198-201).

The parody brings Bassanio back to the solemnity of the recent wedding vows, yet she continues by moving the spotlight back onto the 'lawyer's demand for the ring, insisting that she doesn't believe it. The sequence tests Bassanio's powers of explanation to the full.

value (perhaps also "power" deriving from the magical properties of the stones)

retain

ardent devotion

would be shameless enough to insist on receiving something so sacred

208-236 On one level Portia hears Bassanio speak the truth, and there will be honesty in their relationship. But is this at the cost of Bassanio's friendship with Antonio proving the stronger force? Is there comedy in Bassanio's swearing by the star when we

doctor of civil law (perhaps with a pun on civil = "polite")

And suffered° him to go displeased away,
Even he that had held up° the very life
Of my dear friend. What should I say, sweet lady?
I was enforced to send it after him,
I was beset with shame and courtesy,°
My honor would not let ingratitude
So much besmear it. Pardon me, good lady,
For by these blessed candles° of the night,
Had you been there, I think you would have begged
The ring of me to give the worthy doctor.

PORTIA Let not that doctor e'er come near my house.
Since he hath got the jewel that I loved
And that which you did swear to keep for me,
I will become as liberal° as you,
I'll not deny him anything I have,
No, not my body nor my husband's bed.
Know him° I shall, I am well sure of it.
Lie not a night from home. Watch me like Argos.°
If you do not, if I be left alone,
Now by mine honor which is yet mine own,°
I'll have that doctor for my bedfellow.

NERISSA And I his clerk. Therefore be well advised°
How you do leave me to mine own protection.

GRATIANO Well, do you so. Let not me take° him then,
For if I do, I'll mar the young clerk's pen.°

ANTONIO I am th'unhappy subject of these quarrels.

PORTIA Sir, grieve not you, you are welcome notwithstanding.

BASSANIO Portia, forgive me this enforced wrong,°
And in the hearing of these many friends
I swear to thee, even by thine own fair eyes,
Wherein I see myself—

PORTIA Mark you but that?
In both my eyes he doubly sees himself,
In each eye one. Swear by your double° self,
And there's an oath of credit.°

BASSANIO Nay, but hear me.

allowed

saved

assailed by feelings of shame and obligations of courtesy

stars

1) prodigal 2) sexually free

i.e. sexually

the hundred-eyed monster of classical myth

intact, as well as the usual sense

very careful

get hold of

pen is a sexual pun

fault I was obliged to commit

with a pun on "double-dealing"

ironic: "That's very likely to be believed!"

know it is a cloudy dawn? Is the artifice of his Petrarchan mode being mocked? just as Portia parodied his rhetoric?

Bassanio begins to squirm. Although funny to the audience, to the characters on stage the dialogue must seem hard. The production can portray Portia's knowingness as play or something more difficult. She takes the quarrel a step further and as Bassanio gave up the jewel for Antonio's body, so she will give her body to the 'doctor' for the jewel. When she shows the ring meant faithfulness and trust to her and what she would be prepared to do when that trust is broken, the poetic language underlines the seriousness of the debate. The tension of the scene derives from the way it plays seriousness off against humour.

Even in the heat of argument Portia is careful to emphasise that she is still a virgin. This implies that Bassanio has given up his honour, and maybe his body too. Note that throughout the last four speeches neither has dared interrupt the other: on the face of it there is no dialogue, just 'old swearing'.

Attention swings back to the quarrelling between Nerissa and Gratiano, for she is as angry as Portia and has come to the same conclusion. Gratiano, in customary combative style responds with a couplet, whose finality brings thoughts of the scene coming to a close.

237-247 So Antonio's interjection is crucial. It opens the space for Bassanio to ask forgiveness for an action forced on him. Significantly, Bassanio declares his love again, using the same language as 3.2.116-118 and 123-126, but it is now not so well received. Portia interrupts him for the first time. She focuses on his narcissism but breaks off mid-line.

Pardon this fault, and by my soul I'll swear
I never more will break an oath with thee.

ANTONIO I once did lend my body for his wealth,°
Which but for him that had your husband's ring
Had quite miscarried. I dare be bound again,
My soul upon the forfeit, that your lord
Will never more break faith advisedly.°

PORTIA Then you shall be his surety.° Give him this,
And bid him keep it better than the other.

ANTONIO Here, Lord Bassanio, swear to keep this ring.

BASSANIO By heaven, it is the same I gave the doctor!

PORTIA I had it of him. Pardon me, Bassanio,
For by this ring the doctor lay with me.
Nerissa. And pardon me, my gentle Gratiano,
For that same scrubbed boy the doctor's clerk,
In lieu of° this, last night did lie with me.

GRATIANO Why, this is like the mending of highways
In summer where the ways are fair enough.°
What, are we cuckolds° ere we have deserved it?

PORTIA Speak not so grossly. You are all amazed.
Here is a letter, read it at your leisure;
It comes from Padua from Bellario.
There you shall find that Portia was the doctor,
Nerissa there her clerk. Lorenzo here
Shall witness I set forth as soon as you,
And even but now returned; I have not yet
Entered my house. Antonio, you are welcome,
And I have better news in store for you
Than you expect: unseal this letter soon,°
There shall you find three of your argosies
Are richly come to harbor suddenly.
You shall not know by what strange accident
I chanced on this letter.

ANTONIO I am dumb.

BASSANIO Were you the doctor, and I knew you not?

well-being

knowingly

pledge

248-264 Antonio understands this is about him. He interjects a second time, and raises the stakes when he says that Bassanio will never knowingly break faith again with Portia. As he speaks for Bassanio so Antonio is giving him up. As he stands surety for Bassanio so Antonio recognises Portia's interest in him. Bassanio is at liberty to give up Antonio.

When Portia gives Antonio the ring, it is almost a second wedding where he is asked to give the bridegroom away by the bride. When Bassanio receives the ring he is amazed, and can say nothing for the next twenty-two lines. To add to his disquiet Portia asks for his forgiveness for lying with the 'doctor' and that her 'doctor' was a lie. Nerissa goads Gratiano, calling him 'gentle' when we knows he flies off the handle, taunting him with her ring in the same way as Portia. Taking his cue Gratiano becomes argumentative and attacks.

return for

i.e. instead of in winter when they really need it; "this is like being punished before we've done anything wrong"

husbands whose wives have been unfaithful

265-287 Portia takes great offence and gives Bassanio a letter. As he opens and reads it, so she summarises and invokes Lorenzo as witness.

Are Gratiano and Bassanio reading the letter together? As they read, Portia gives one to Antonio and tells him its contents. The play acknowledges the difficulty of any realistic explanation and has Portia say that she will not divulge 'by what strange accident' she came on the news.

quickly

Antonio may be silent but Bassanio and Gratiano are dumfounded. Nerissa immediately replies to their questions, but Portia does not. Bassanio speaks again, trying to build on the other couple's reconciliation, yet Portia does not reply. Antonio finishes reading his letter and accepts it as proof of what she said.

GRATIANO Were you the clerk that is to make me cuckold?

NERISSA Ay, but the clerk that never means to do it,
Unless he live until he be a man.

BASSANIO Sweet doctor, you shall be my bedfellow.
When I am absent, then lie with my wife.

ANTONIO Sweet lady, you have given me life and living,
For here I read for certain that my ships
Are safely come to road.°

PORTIA How now, Lorenzo?
My clerk hath some good comforts too for you.

NERISSA Ay, and I'll give them him without a fee.
There do I give to you and Jessica
From the rich Jew a special deed of gift
After his death, of all he dies possessed of.

LORENZO Fair ladies, you drop manna in the way
Of starved people.°

PORTIA It is almost morning,
And yet I am sure you are not satisfied
Of these events at full.° Let us go in,
And charge us there upon inter'gatories,°
And we will answer all things faithfully.

GRATIANO Let it be so. The first inter'gatory
That my Nerissa shall be sworn on is,
Whether till the next night she had rather stay,°
Or go to bed now, being two hours to day.
But were the day come, I should wish it dark
Till I were couching with the doctor's clerk.
Well, while I live I'll fear no other thing°
So sore, as keeping safe Nerissa's ring.° Exeunt.

FINIS.

harbor

bread which rained from heaven to feed the Israelites in the wilderness (Exodus 16)

fully how all these events happened

swear under oath to answer all necessary questions; Portia reverts to a bit of legal jargon

wait

the same pun as "pen" l.236 above

with a pun on "vagina"

288-306 Portia still delays answering Bassanio by turning her attention to Lorenzo. Is Lorenzo upset, since Portia says 'How now Lorenzo?'.

He and Jessica have been silently on the periphery, and now Nerissa gives him the deed of gift. Note that Antonio, perhaps because he is self-absorbed, chooses not to tell Lorenzo and Jessica about his half of Shylock's money. Although Nerissa includes Jessica, she remains silent. Is she still unresolved about her relationship with her father? Lorenzo speaks for them both.

Most productions forget about Shylock once he leaves the courtroom. Jude Kelly's West Yorkshire Playhouse production kept his presence alive. John Peter writes "This ending, when Hebrew music is played on the terraces at Belmont and Jessica sobs with remorse, anguish and joy, is deep and unexpectedly moving" (Sunday Times, 1994).

A production has to choose how Portia and Bassanio use body language with each other here. Is it relaxed or constrained? It has been 40 lines since she has said anything to him. Portia notes that it is just before morning, and her lines at 294-295 can either be taken at face value or problematised because she knows there is more to find out about the interrelationship between herself, Bassanio and Antonio.

Given Bassanio's silence, Gratiano's speech speaks for them both as he leaps into a joyously sexual rhyming couplet. Will it remain a cloudy day, or turn sunny? The production is left to decide as Portia, Bassanio, Antonio and all exit.

Bibliography

Brandel, Betty. "Ellen Terry's Foul Papers," *Theatre Survey*, 10 (1969): 43-52.

Barton, John, *Playing Shakespeare* (London and New York, 1984).

Berry, Ralph, ed., *On Directing Shakespeare* (London, 1972).

Brockbank, Philip, ed., *Players of Shakespeare* (Cambridge and New York, 1985).

Brown, John Russell, "The Realization of Shylock," *Early Shakespeare* (London, 1966), pp. 187-209.

— "Three Directors," *Shakespeare Survey*, 14 (1961): 129-37

— , ed., *The Merchant of Venice*, Arden edn (London, 1961).

Cook, Judith, *Women in Shakespeare* (London, 19980).

Esselin, Martin, "*The Merchant of Venice*," *Plays and Players*, 19 no.11 (1972): 44-5.

Faucit, Helen, *On Some of Shakespeare's Female Characters* (Edinburgh, 1885).

Foulkes, Richard, "Helen Faucit and Ellen Terry as Portia," *Theatre Notebook*, 331 (1977): 27-37

— , "Henry Irving and Lawrence Olivier as Shylock," *Theatre Notebook*, 27 (1973): 26-36

Furness, H.H. ed. *The Merchant of Venice*, Variorum edn. (Philadelphia, 1888).

Hawkins, F.W., *The Life of Edmund Kean*, 2 vols. (London, 1869).

Hazlin, William, *Characters of Shakespeare's Plays* (1817; London, 1920).

Hicks, Sir Seymour, *Hail Fellow Well Met* (London, 1949).

Hole, Richard, "An Apology for the Character and Conduct of Shylock," *Essays by a Society of Gentlemen at Exeter* (London, 1796).

James, Henry, *The Scenic Art*, ed. Allan Wade (London, 1949).

Kirkman, J.T., *Memoirs of Macklin*, 2 vols. (London, 1799).

Leggatt, Alexander, *Shakespeare's Comedy of Love* (London and New York, 1974), pp. 117-150.

Lelyveld, Toby, *Shakespeare on Stage* (Cleveland, 1960).

Levin, Harry, "A Garden in Belmont," *Shakespeare and Dramatic Tradition*, ed. W.R. Elton and William B. Long (London, 1989), pp. 13-31.

Lyon, John, *The Merchant of Venice* (Hemel Hampstead, 1988).

Mahood, M.M. ed. *The Merchant of Venice*, New Cambridge edn. (Cambridge, 1987).

Marowitz, Charles, *Variations on The Merchant of Venice* (1977).

Mennen, Richard E., "Theodore Komisarjevsky's Production of *The Merchant of Venice,*" *The Theatre Journal* 31 (1979): 386-97.

Moody, A.D., *Shakespeare: The Merchant of Venice* (London, 1964).

Overton, Bill, *The Merchant of Venice* (London, 1987).

Poel, William, *Shakespeare in the Theatre* (London and Toronto, 1913).

Speaight, Robert, *William Poel and the Elizabethan Revival* (London, 1954).

— , "The 1960 Season at Stratford-upon-Avon," *Shakespeare Quarterly*, 11 (1960): 445-53.

Terry, Ellen, *Four Lectures on Shakespeare* (London, 1912)

— , *The Story of My Life* (London, 1908). Warren, Roger, "A Year of Comedies: Stratford 1978," *Shakespeare Survey*, 32 (1979): 201-9,

Wesker, Arnold, *The Merchant* (1980).

Winter, William, *The Life and Art of Edwin Booth* (New York, 1874),

— , *Shakespeare on the Stage* (New York, 1912).

SOURCES AND BACKGROUND

Besides discussions in the editions by Furness, Brown and Mahood cited above, Geoffrey Bullough's *Narrative and Dramatic Sources of Shakespeare, vol. 1* (London, 1964) reprints all the major sources and introduces them, while Christopher Spencer's *The Genesis of Shakespeare's Merchant of Venice* (Lewiston, N.Y., 1989) traces their original literary and social contexts.

FURTHER READING

Barnet, Sylvan, ed., *Twentieth-Century Interpretations of The Merchant of Venice* (Englewood Cliffs, N.J., 1970).

Bloom, Alan, ed., *Modern Critical Interpretations: Shakespeare's The Merchant of Venice* (New York, 1986).

Brown, John Russell, "*The Merchant of Venice*," *Shakespeare and His Comedies* (London, 1957), pp. 45-81.

Carson, Neil, "Hazarding and Cozening in *The Merchant of Venice*," *English Language Notes*, 9 (1972): 168-77.

Coghill, Nevill, "The Basis of Shakespearian Comedy," *Shakespearian Criticism 1935-1960*, ed. Anne Ridler (Oxford, 1963).

Cohen, D.M., "The Jew and Shylock," *Shakespeare Quarterly*, 31 (1980):

Cohen, Walter, "*The Merchant of Venice* and the Possibilities of Historical Criticism," *English Literary History*, 49 (1982): 765-89.

Danson, Lawrence, *The Harmonies of The Merchant of Venice* (New Haven, 1978).

Dessen, Alan C., "The Elizabethan Stage Jew and Christian Example," *Modern Language Quarterly*, 35 (1974): 231-45.

Geary, Keith, "The Nature of Portia's Victory: Turning to Men in *The Merchant of Venice*," *Shakespeare Survey*, 37 (1984): 55-68.

Hill, .F., "*The Merchant of Venice* and the Pattern of Romantic Comedy," *Shakespeare Survey*, 28 (1975): 75-87.

Jordan, William Chester, "Approaches to the Court Scene in *The Merchant of Venice*," *Shakespeare Quarterly*, 33 (1982): 49-59.

Midgley, Graham, "*The Merchant of Venice*: A Reconsideration," *Essays in Criticism*, 10 (1960): 119-33.

Newman, Karen, "Portia's Ring: Unruly Women and Structures of Exchange in *The Merchant of Venice*," *Shakespeare Quarterly*, 38 (1987): 19-33.

Rabkin, Norman, "Meaning and *The Merchant of Venice*," *Shakespeare and the Problem of Meaning* (Chicago and London, 1981).

Shapiro, Michael, "Shylock the Jew Onstage: Past and Present," *Shofar*, 4.2 (1986): 1-11.

Speaight, Robert, *Shakespeare on the Stage* (London, 1973).

Sprague, A.C., *Shakespeare and the Actors* (Cambridge, Mass., 1944), pp. 19-31.

Tennenhouse, Leonard, *Power on Display* (New York, 1986), pp. 52-61.

Wilders, John, ed., *Shakespeare: The Merchant of Venice*, Casebook Series (London and Basingstoke, 1968).

Textual Notes

Copy-text for this edition:	the first Quarto, printed 1600 (Q1)
Other texts:	the second Quarto, printed 1619 (Q2) the First Folio, printed 1623 (F)
Abbreviations and symbols:	**s.d.** stage direction ^ omission **s.p.** speech prefix

The list below records this edition's major departures (that is, those involving substantive differences in meaning) from the original and only authoritative edition of the play, Q1. Since both Q2 and F derive from Q1, they lack independent authority, although F contains certain stage directions absent in Q1 which may derive from the staging of the play in Shakespeare's day (e.g. II.i.0.1 s.d. "[Flourish of cornets.]" Some of these directions are included in this edition and appear, like other editorial additions, in square brackets. Other minor changes, such as corrections of typographical errors and mislineation, or modernization of spellings and punctuation, have been made silently. This edition's reading appears first in italics, followed by the Q1 reading (in original spelling).

I.i. 0.1 s.d. [and elsewhere in this edition] *SALERIO, and SOLANIO* SALARYNO, and SALANIO 19 *Peering* [F] Piring 27 *docked* docks 114 *Yet* it

I.ii. 51 *throstle* Trassell 101.1 s.d. *Enter a SERVINGMAN* after "what newes?" in Q1

I.iii. 25 s.p. [*and elsewhere in this edition*] *SHYLOCK* Iew 105 *spit* spet 118 *spat* spet 123 *spit* spet

II.i. 0.1 s.d. *MOROCHUS* MOROCCO 31 *the Lady* thee, lady

II.ii. 1 s.p. [*and elsewhere in this edition*] *LAUNCELOT* CLOWNE 3 [*and elsewhere in this edition*] *GOBBO* Iobbe 9 *heavens,* heavens^ 96.1 s.d. *Enter...two* after "any longer" in Q1 153.1 s.d. *Exit LEONARDO* after "done heerein" in Q1 156 *have a* [Q2, F] haue ^

II.iv. 8 s.d. *Enter LAUNCELOT* after "newes" in Q1 13 *Love-news* Loue, newes 19.1 *Exit...clown* after "Torch-bearer" in Q1 26 s.d. *Exeunt* Exit 38 s.d. *Exeunt* Exit

II.vi. 24 *therein* then 25 *Ho,* [Q2] Howe 57 *gentlemen* [Q2, F] gentleman

II.vii. 18 *threatens.* threatens^ 45 *Spits* Spets 70 *tombs* timber

II.viii. 39 *Slubber* [Q2, F] slumber

II.ix. 100 *Lord Love* Lord, loue

III.i. 16.1 s.d. *Enter SHYLOCK* after "the MERCHANTS?" in Q1 64.1 s.d. *Enter TUBAL* Q1 repeats this direction after "Exeunt GENTLEMEN." 89 *Heard* heere

III.ii. 61 *live.* liue^ 67 *eyes* [F] eye 81 *vice* voyce 93 *make* maketh 204 *roof* [Q2] rough 216.1 s.d. *Enter...Venice* after "friend SALERIO?" in Q1

III.iii. 0.1 s.d. *SOLANIO* [F] SALERIO

III.iv. 49 *Padua* Mantua 50 *cousin's* [Q2, F] cosin 53 *traject* Tranect

III.v. 19 *e'en* [Q2, F] in 24 *comes* [Q2, F] come? 68 *merit it* meane it, it 75 *for a* [F] for ^

IV.i. 30 *his state* [Q2, F] this states 36 *Sabbath* [Q2, F] Sabaoth 50 *urine; for* vrine^ for 51 *MISTRESS* MAISTERS 73 *You may as well* [Q1 corrected, Q2] ^ ^ ^ well 74 *Why he hath made the* [Q1 corrected, Q2,] ^ ^ ^ ^ the *bleat* [F] bleake 75 *mountain pines* [F] mountaine of Pines 100 *'tis* [Q2, F] as 162.1 s.d. *disguised as* for 226 *No, not* [Q2, F] Not not 281 *I*^ ay, 318 *off* of 393 s.p. *GRATIANO* [Q2, F] SHY[LOCK]

V.i. 41 *MASTER LORENZO?* [Calls] M. LORENZO, & 48 *Sweet soul* assigned in Q1 to the previous speech after "ere morning"

50 *STEPHANO* [Q2] STEPHEN 55 *ears; soft stillness*^ eares^ soft stilnes, 86 *EREBUS* TEREBUS 151 *give it* [Q2, F] giue ^ 232 *my* [Q2, F] mine

Peter Lichtenfels

Commentary: *The Merchant of Venice*

A theatre director for over thirty years, both in Europe and North America, Peter Lichtenfels has also been Artistic Director of the Traverse Theatre, Edinburgh, and Executive Director of the Leicester Haymarket. Over the past ten years he has increasingly turned his attention to Shakespeare's plays and has directed among others, *Romeo and Juliet*, *Anthony and Cleopatra* and *Richard III*, as well as *The Merchant of Venice*. Currently combining directing with teaching acting at Manchester Metropolitan University (England), he is co-editing *Romeo and Juliet* for the Arden Third Series.

Randall Martin

Editor: *The Merchant of Venice*

Randall Martin is currently an Associate Professor in the Department of English at the University of New Brunswick. He received a BA (with distinction) for English at Trinity College of the University of Toronto, before completing his studies for an MA in Shakespeare Studies at the University of Birmingham's Shakespeare Institute. Randall Martin has also attained a DPhil in English from Merton College at the University of Oxford.

In his editorial career, his works include *Henry VI Part Three*, The Oxford Shakespeare and Oxford Classics, to be published by Oxford University Press, U.K (July 2001), *Women Writers in Renaissance England*, by Longmans, U.K (1997), *Edmond Ironside*, and Anthony Brewer's *The Love-sick King* by Garland Press, N.Y (1991). He is currently working on *Women's Crime Pamphlets and News Broadsides 1500-1640*, in Series III of *The Early Modern Englishwoman, a facsimile library of essential works*, to be released by Ashgate/Scholar Press, New York (2002).

SOLILOQUY!

The Shakespeare Monologues

Edited by Michael Earley and Philippa Keil

At last, over 175 of Shakespeare's finest and most performable monologues taken from all 37 plays are here in two easy-to-use volumes (MEN and WOMEN). Selections travel the entire spectrum of the great dramatist's vision, from comedies and romances to tragedies, pathos and histories.

"Soliloquy is an excellent and comprehensive collection of Shakespeare's speeches. Not only are the monologues wide-ranging and varied, but they are superbly annotated. Each volume is prefaced by an informative and reassuring introduction, which explains the signals and signposts by which Shakespeare helps an actor on his journey through the text. It includes a very good explanation of blank verse, with excellent examples of irregularities which are specifically related to character and acting intentions. These two books are a must for any actor in search of a 'classical' audition piece."

ELIZABETH SMITH
Head of Voice & Speech
The Juilliard School

paper•MEN: ISBN 0-936839-78-3
WOMEN: ISBN 0936839-79-1

APPLAUSE